DEGREES
Of
SUCCESS

DEGREES

Of

SUCCESS

INSPIRING STORIES AND SECRETS TO SUCCESS

"I went from secretary to president in 4 years
without a college degree."

CLAUDIA FOX

ISBN: 978-1-63649-234-6   (Paperback Edition)
ISBN: 978-1-63649-235-3   (Hardcover Edition)
ISBN: 978-1-63649-233-9   (E-book Edition)

Book Ordering Information

Phone Number: 315 288-7939 ext. 1000 or 347-901-4920
Email: info@globalsummithouse.com
Global Summit House
www.globalsummithouse.com

Printed in the United States of America

"*Our deepest fear is not that we are inadequate, our deepest fear is that we are powerful beyond measure. It is our light, not our darkness that most frightens us. We ask ourselves, who am I to be brilliant, gorgeous, talented and fabulous? Actually who are you not to be? You are a child of God. Your playing small doesn't serve the World. There is nothing enlightened about shrinking so that other people won't feel insecure around you. We are born to manifest our glory that is within us. It is not just in some of us, it is in everyone. And as we let our own light shine, we unconsciously give other people permission to do the same. As we are liberated from our fear, our presence automatically liberates others.*"

Marianne Williamson
Author "A Return to Love"

ACKNOWLEDGMENTS

My special thanks to all of the following:

My son, Ryan Fox, whom I love dearly and who always inspires me to make the world a better place. Ryan's fiancé, Jacqui Marcos, who is the daughter I never had and who has always been encouraging of my work.

Susan Hyatt who has held my handout throughout my journey to arrive at this wonderful place of light and love.

My sisters and brothers: Laura, George, Susan, Ginny, Karl; their spouses: Gary, John, Tuyen; their families: Brandon/Karel, Ethan; Erik, Elliot, Josh/Kelly, Kaden, Renner and Rex/Erica, Gustavo for their love and strong family foundation. A special thanks to Victoria Guglielmi who gave me the courage I needed to move forward with this project as well as create a wonderful website for my coaching practice.

My incredible friends, Patricia Keenan, Christy Record and Peter Bittner, who walked me through many of the spiritual and financial steps leading to publishing my book. Maureen Chatfield, a creative genius and life-long friend, Laura Banks, a friend with a wealth of ideas, Josephine and Daryl Adams for their unconditional love. Terry Ferraro, who has supplied me people for my book. Paul Turro who created the space for me to realize I could do this, Clive Swersky, who has been a steadfast supporter of my visions and goals. My "Wisdom" crew: Carey Samuels-Hochberg, Leonard Birbrower, Robert DiVincenzo, Karen McLean, Gordon Updegraff, Mark Smith, Andrew Rice, Malcolm

Williams, and Andre Wallace, who became the family that taught me I could have it all.

Robert Allen and Mark Victor Hansen for imparting their wisdom and being such awesome role models.

CONTENTS

PREFACE

"You've got a lot of street smarts, kid, but you need a college degree to succeed in business." How many times have you been told this by prospective employers who shut the door in your face after learning you never attended, or didn't finish college? The stigma of lacking a college diploma could have dashed your dreams for a successful career—sending them straight out the door and into the trash bin. But wait, you're intelligent, highly motivated, and you like to take risks! It's not that college didn't cross your mind; perhaps you didn't have the funds, or maybe you just didn't want to put your ideas on hold while you were sitting in a stuffy classroom for four years. So why should you be penalized?

While it is true there are times when a college degree gets you in the door and pushes you up the ladder more quickly, there's a lot more to be said for self-motivation. Take Bill Gates, Richard Branson, and Ted Turner—all were college dropouts. So eager was Peter Jennings to jumpstart his career that he dropped out of preparatory school and headed straight for the news desk. And, world-renowned poet Maya Angelou didn't finish high school. People who achieve success without a college degree have many traits in common: the will to succeed and the tenacity and confidence to do what it takes to achieve their goals. They are risk-takers who are not afraid to seize opportunities, regardless of their skills and experience. When asked if they can do something, they first say "yes" and then figure out how to do it. Bill Gates, for example, promised to deliver the BASIC computer code that would revolutionize personal computers before he'd even written it; BASIC then became the first computer program ever written for a PC.

These people keep a positive attitude and consider adversity no more than a stepping stone on the road to success. They thrive on instinct and common sense, along with the ability to surround themselves with people of similar optimism.

.   Success comes not only from having particular skills, but also from an impassioned desire to achieve more. Most average academics couldn't even begin to tackle what Ted Turner does; being a high-energy entrepreneur takes a very different mindset than being a college professor. For entrepreneurs, there's no time like the present. They are out there learning on the job, constantly figuring out how to bank roll their ideas.

In "DEGREES OF SUCCESS, "I went from secretary to president in 4 years without a college degree" People Reveal Secrets to Their Success! You will meet a few of the people who have made significant contributions to society without a college diploma. Some of their names are well known, but the stories of people who are not so famous—such as one-time bank clerk Betty Flores who became Mayor of Laredo, Texas, and Steven J. Belmonte, president and CEO of Hospitality Solutions, or real estate entrepreneur Fenton Soliz—are equally compelling and inspirational. These are real people who have realized their goals regardless of background, obstacles, and pitfalls. They are all incredible self-made success stories, and not one has a college degree.

There are over 5 million millionaires in the United States, and many of them are self-made. Even Donald Trump, who holds a graduate degree from the prestigious Wharton School and is arguably one of the most successful businessmen in the world, has recognized the value and potential of people without a college education. In the third season of his highly acclaimed reality show "The Apprentice," non-college graduates competed against college grads for a coveted position within the Trump Organization.

We've already mentioned Peter Jennings and Bill Gates, two of the most extraordinary and widely recognized non-graduates. Born in Toronto, Ontario, the son of a leading journalist, announcer, and later executive with the Canadian Broadcasting Company, Jennings not only did not attend college, he didn't even graduate from high school.

Starting young, at age nine, he hosted a half-hour weekly children's show on CBS called "Peter's Place." As a young man, he had no fear and set out to create what he wanted. He became an interviewer for an

Ontario radio station after dropping out of preparatory school, then joined the CBC as host of a public-affairs program. In 1962, he became co-anchor of Canada's first national commercial-network newscast, then moved to New York in 1964 and worked as a correspondent for ABC, becoming anchor of ABC Nightly News in 1965 at the age of 26—the youngest person ever to have held that prestigious position.

His colleagues, however, were not happy that he was so inexperienced, and he was let go because he could not compete with Walter Cronkite of CBS and David Brinkley of NBC, the two most respected anchors of that time. Yet he persevered. ABC sent him overseas as a foreign correspondent, and it has often been said that his work in the trenches gave him the base of experience that has made him such a compassionate interviewer.

He did what was necessary to take him to the next level and went on to anchor ABC's World News Tonight for nearly 20 years, becoming one of the most recognizable faces and names in the media today. His many awards include the National Headliner Award for his reporting on the Civil War in Bangladesh, a Peabody Award in 1974 for his profile of Egyptian president Anwar al-Sadat, and 12 national Emmy Awards. It is estimated that his contract with ABC now brings him between $7 to $9 million a year.

Peter is a great example of someone who took advantage of his upbringing, his talent, and his connections. He admits he was a terrible student, but he did have a childhood hero, Thomas Edison, the inventor, because he was a self-made man. His message to the younger generation is, "Be humble and have a sense of humor, you will need it."

Bill Gates, another world-famous self-starter, dropped out of Harvard, and with his partner and fellow drop-out, Paul Allen, went on to found Microsoft and commercialize software for the personal computer, which was then in its infancy.

Gates has been quoted as saying, "I have infinite amounts of money," but he and his company went through tough times along the way. After about seven years of complaints, cold reviews, insincere compliments, and sluggish sales, the Microsoft Windows operating system was spiraling downward. As the only one left of the original young microcomputer pioneers and the only one left in control of his original company, Bill stepped up to the plate and publicized what the new Windows could do: switch between programs and paste or "hot-link" them together. There were colors, fancier icons, cleaner borders, and better choices of fonts, and you could write really big programs. With this new publicity, customers were waiting outside software stores' front doors to buy it, and by the end of the first year, Windows 3.0 sold more than 4 million units, ensuring Microsoft's success.

Gates grew up a nerdy, goofy, high-energy kid with two sisters and a loving mother and father. Often late, he would tell his parents, "I'm thinking, I'm thinking." And when they pressured him to be on time, he asked them, "Don't you ever think?" He was very industrious, and in the sixth grade he was included in a special economics class for which he prepared a report entitled "Invest with Gateway Incorporated." In his report, Bill imagined himself to be a "young inventor" marketing a coronary care system to hospitals. He wrote, "I am going to incorporate in order to avoid personal liabilities." He addressed issues, such as raising sufficient capital, hiring management, hiring skilled workers and a sales force. He concluded, "If my idea is good and I am able to hire good people and raise enough money, I should be successful. Even in the sixth grade, he was thinking in a "big picture" entrepreneurial way. Gates received an A on his report, but he wasn't happy about it. In fact, he often tried to hide how smart he was so that he'd feel more included and used to tell his teacher that he actually didn't deserve such a good grade because his desk was too messy. He was, however, competitive in other ways and enjoyed playing games like "Risk," whose goal is to "take over the world." Obviously Bill was even then preparing for his future.

There are many other famous and not-so-famous people who have climbed to the top using their talents and skills without a college degree. T. Harv Eker, President of Peak Potential Training, the fastest growing personal development company in North America, and #1 NY Times best-selling author of Secrets of the Millionaire Mind, went from having nothing to becoming a millionaire in only 21/2 years! He combines a unique brand of "street smarts with heart" and now teaches several highly acclaimed courses, including The Millionaire.

Among other such success stories are Richard Branson, billionaire mogul and TV show host, Barbara Corcoran, founder and Chairman of the Corcoran Group who sold her business for $74 million dollars, attorney David Boies, Jesse Ventura, the former governor of Minnesota, Andrew Carnegie, Coco Chanel, Walter Cronkite, Michael Dell, founder of Dell computers, Walt Disney, Thomas Alva Edison, Ben Franklin, S. B. Fuller, founder of the Fuller-Brush company, Ernest Hemingway, Milton Hershey, founder of Hershey Chocolates, astronaut and Senator John Glenn, Barry Goldwater, Ralph Lauren, Abraham Lincoln, Charles Lindbergh, Clare Booth Luce, playwright Neil Simon, John D. Rockefeller, David Sarnoff, Harry S. Truman, Ted Turner, Mark Twain, George Washington, Thomas J. Watson, founder of IBM, inventor George Westinghouse, poet Walt Whitman, Steve Wozniak, co-founder of Apple Computers, aeronautics pioneer Orville Wright, John Smith, the Chairman of General Motors, and Edward Rensi, President of McDonald's USA.

The meaning of all these success stories is that you can do what you want to do. Yes, there may be obstacles along the way, but if you point yourself in the right direction, begin talking about your goal, and enroll people in supporting you, the sky is the limit.

To order DEGREES OF SUCCESS, view live interviews, blog or contact Claudia Fox:
Go to www.thefoxwayworks.com

I have known for more than ten years that I would one day interview people and write a book, but being the "type A" personality that I am, I was always too busy. Then I became very ill. After three and a half years, I was finally diagnosed with lyme disease. It was a very difficult time for me, but as I began my recovery, I was able to get in touch with my "dharma" or purpose in life, which I discovered is to motivate and help people become successful— especially those without a college degree. I believe whole-heartedly that every experience happens for a reason, and the lyme disease provided me with the time to breathe and think about where I was going in my life. Over the past year and a half, I have been blessed with one person after another who volunteered to be interviewed for this book. Between these pages, you will meet some of those wonderful people.

MY STORY

Claudia Fox

I was born and grew up in the Midwest, the eldest of six children. My father's philosophy of education was that "boys go to college and girls have babies," and that certainly seemed to be what my mother did because, to me, it appeared that she was always pregnant. My father ran the household with an iron fist, and my mother was expected to do whatever he asked. In fact, my father and mother spent most of their marriage—which ultimately lasted forty-five years until his death— arguing and talking about divorce. In that atmosphere, and with so many younger siblings and babies around, it was difficult for me to get much attention. As a result, I found it difficult to be assertive, but I did discover my strengths: being smart, friendly, and nice.

During my first four years of elementary school, I was a popular kid and got straight A's. And then my father announced that we were moving "to a big city far away from here." As it turned out, the new city was only about an hour away, but at my age, it might as well have been another world.

At first I was excited about the move, but when I told my fourth-grade teacher, her response was to say, "Claudia, don't think you're going to be smart in your new school." That really shocked me, and as I played it over and over in my head through the years to come, it became more and more true. As it turned out, the kids in my new elementary school were not only ahead of me academically, they were also more affluent, and I always felt that I just wasn't good enough and would never catch up. To make up for my insecurities and "fit in," I developed what is generally called a pleasing personality.

When I reached high school, there were two "tracks" that I could follow. The academic track was the direct route to college, and the business track offered courses such as typing and shorthand. Since it had already been drummed into my head by my father that a woman's greatest aspiration ought to be to become a secretary and then "graduate" to becoming a devoted housewife and mother, I, of course, followed the business track. And I found out that I was good at it.

After graduation, I got my first job as a secretary, and I remained a secretary, at one place or another, for the next twelve years—not particularly because I wanted to, but because I just couldn't figure out what I needed to do to get ahead like others were.

My big breakthrough—really the turning point in my life—interestingly came not through what I had learned on the job, but through social experience. By that time, I'd moved to New York City, and I'd met a young man at the office whom I began to date. Very early in the relationship, however, he informed me in no uncertain terms that if we were going to continue seeing one another, I'd have to learn to ski because that's what he did every weekend during the winter months.

I was game to try. I even committed to joining his "ski house" in Vermont, but, in fact, I was miserable. It was a four-hour drive every Friday night, and then everyone was up bright and early the next morning to hit the slopes. Putting on all those layers of clothes was a chore, and no matter how many layers I wore, I was always cold. By the time I got to the slope, I was in tears. And, since all the others had been skiing for years, they headed up to the top of the mountain while I was relegated to the beginner's or "bunny" slope for lessons.

To order DEGREES OF SUCCESS, view live interviews, blog or contact Claudia Fox:
Go to www.thefoxwayworks.com

It was a tough winter for me, but I was determined to get up to the top of that mountain and join the rest of the group. After a month, I announced that I was ready. The others were doubtful, but I insisted. After only three runs, I plowed right into two other skiers and was taken off the mountain on a stretcher with pulled ligaments that kept me in a cast for a week. But I was still determined, and just two weeks after the cast came off, I was back on the mountain. After a few more lessons, I finally "got it."

The group had already planned to go to Aspen the following spring for a skiing vacation, and when we got there, I headed right for the slopes with the others. In fact, on that very first weekend, I started volunteering to teach beginners. It turned out to be a great vacation, and as the years have gone on, I've become an expert skier.

What the experience taught me, however, was that if I had a goal, I might not like everything I had to do to achieve it, but doing those things would ultimately build my confidence and get me closer to where I wanted to be. The "bonus" for me was discovering that I could also pass along what I'd learned to others and take pride in their achievements. These were lessons that I'd use in my business life from that point on.

Once I'd discovered my own power, I began to use my experience to advance my career. One of my secretarial jobs had been with KLM Airlines, and I now built on my skills and the knowledge I'd accumulated about the airline industry to go from secretary to account executive to director of sales and marketing for an airline uniform company. Within six or seven years, I was earning in the top one percent of all women in the country.

After having worked for the airlines for several years, I became interested in real estate and secured a position as a secretary with Sotheby Parke Bernet Real Estate. I worked for twelve women in the real estate department while attending classes to become a sales agent. Once I was licensed, and after completing my commitment, I began to sell high-end properties. Starting at the lower end of the spectrum, I worked my way up over the next two years to selling million-dollar residences, including Lee Radziwell's (Jackie Kennedy Osassis's sister) Park Avenue apartment. However, working on commission was difficult for me, and I, therefore, expressed an interest in a new condominium project Sotheby's had taken on. I sold 35 units and, through that experience, became an expert in condominium projects. Subsequently, I was hired by Donald Trump to work on Trump Plaza in New York City. As I'd learned along the way, one experience generally leads to the next, and as a result of the Trump project, I was hired by Manhattan Sales, a joint venture between William Zeckendorf and Worldwide Volkswagen, to lead, train, and motivate the sales agents for their condominium projects. After only four months, I was asked to become president of the organization and was earning an income of well over six figures.

I got married in 1985, and in 1986 I retired from real estate to have my son, Ryan. Since that time I've again worked in real estate and also as a career counselor, inspiring and motivating high-income executives and disadvantaged teens.

In 2003, I co-hosted the cablevision program "Get a Job," and at present I am interviewing guests who have turned their passion into profit on my cablevision program "Alive with Claudia and Clive" Turn Your Passion Into Profit.

What has become clear to me over the years is that the only thing that initially prevented me from achieving success was not the lack of a diploma, but the lack of belief in myself. In the pages that follow, you'll read the stories of others who, like me, have succeeded and thrived in many walks of life without that college degree. Some of them overcame difficult childhoods and used their adversities to strengthen their determination. Some floundered for a while before they found their true passion while others knew from an early age exactly what they wanted to do, and had the courage to go after it. I hope that all their stories will be inspirational, and will give you, too, the courage and passion to follow your dream.

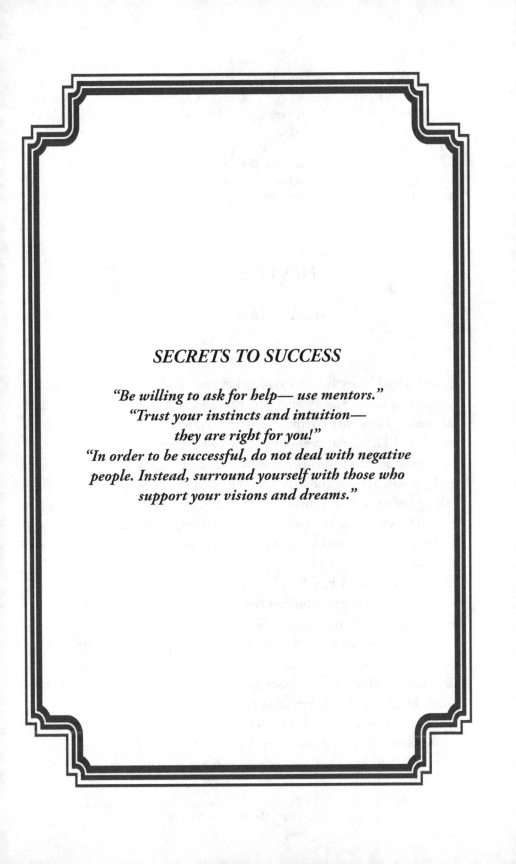

SECRETS TO SUCCESS

"Be willing to ask for help— use mentors."
"Trust your instincts and intuition—
they are right for you!"
"In order to be successful, do not deal with negative
people. Instead, surround yourself with those who
support your visions and dreams."

I always admired Helen Gurley Brown, although I have never personally met her. She has had tremendous courage, and, because of my story, I relate to the way she created her success by working her way up the ladder from secretary to Editor in Chief of Cosmopolitan. When I began working on this book, I called Helen out of the blue, and, much to my surprise, she answered her phone directly. She was incredibly gracious, and working with her on this interview has been wonderful beyond my expectations. Helen and her husband, David Brown, have been married for 45 years.

NEVER SAY NO

Helen Gurley Brown

After Helen Gurley Brown's graduation from high school, she attended Texas State College for Women for one semester, but left to take business courses at Woodbury Business College. Typing and shorthand were the basics and Helen did well—typing 80 words per minute, and taking shorthand at 130 words per minute. She had already secured a job at KHJ Radio Station and was working for a grand $6 per week while taking her secretarial courses.

Since life turned out well, Helen has few regrets about not finishing college. Her career is an unbelievable success story. She knows education is important but her husband says if she had gone to college, it probably would have ruined her! Brought up in a poor family, her sister in a wheelchair, her mother broken-hearted at not being able to send her younger daughter to college, Helen kept soldiering on.

A sore spot in her life, that almost took precedence over every other, was perpetual acne. Jealous of "pretty" women around her, Helen dreamed of being successful. She now feels she is a living example of the good things that happen to good people who try!

After secretarial school, Helen had 17 secretarial jobs before settling in to work for advertising executive Don Belding, partner of Foote, Cone & Belding. They were together for five years. "He is a prince and his wife, Alice, a guardian angel," says Helen. Alice was a feminist. Helen was reasonably happy, and Don wanted to keep her as a secretary but, through his wife's insistence, he gave Helen writing assignments. With some nagging from Alice, Helen "the secretary" was allowed to write Sunkist radio commercials once a year at Christmas.

While working at the agency, Helen entered a Glamour Magazine contest called "Ten Girls with Taste," and was one of the finalists that first year. The second year, Helen was winner of one of the prizes—a wardrobe, and a trip to Hawaii. A question on the entry form had asked: "What do you want to be, what is your ambition?" Though Helen would actually have been happy continuing to work for Don Belding (she was treated like family, taken on vacations, and bought lavish gifts) on the questionnaire she said, "I'd like to be a copywriter." After reading her contest entry, the personnel director of Conde Nast called Don and said, "Why don't you give her a chance?" He did. Helen became a copywriter on the Catalina Swimsuit account where she continued for the next five years. Her hard work and talent paid off, and she became a three-time recipient of the Frances Holmes Advertising Copywriters award.

Working since she was 18, now 37, she had tried writing at various times but was never able to get anything published. Thirty-seven was also when she got married to David Brown, who became a wonderful mentor. He suggested she write a book about her single-girl experience, which would ultimately become the bible for the single woman. "Sex and the Single Girl" debuted in 1962 and became an immediate bestseller. A smashing success, published all over the world, the book became the basis for her revamp of Cosmopolitan magazine and is still considered a publishing phenomenon. Helen, at 83, is editor-in-chief of the international edition of Cosmopolitan—there are 54 editions. Her last book, I'm Wild Again: Snippets From My Life and a Few Brazen Thoughts was published by St. Martin Press in February 2000, and Dear Pussycat in 2004.

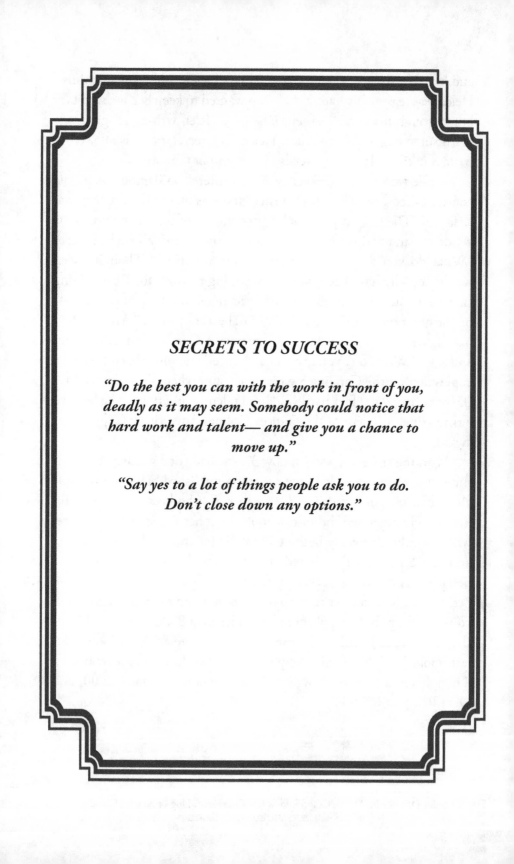

SECRETS TO SUCCESS

*"Do the best you can with the work in front of you,
deadly as it may seem. Somebody could notice that
hard work and talent— and give you a chance to
move up."*

*"Say yes to a lot of things people ask you to do.
Don't close down any options."*

One day I came across a newspaper article about Steven Belmonte. It stated right in the article that he had been successful without a college degree, and, at the time, I remember being amazed by his honesty. When I called to ask if he would participate in my book project, he graciously agreed, but several years went by before I actually got to speak with him again. He remembered who I was and graciously invited me to his beautiful home in New Jersey, where I met him and his lovely wife, and the adorable puppy they were taking care of for a friend. When I saw Steven get down on the floor to play with the puppy, it was a sign to me that he was, indeed, a very special person. He has been married for 21 years and has three children.

PASSION BREEDS SUCCESS

Steven Belmonte

Steven Belmonte was born into a traditional Italian family in Chicago. His mom was a stay-at-home housewife and his father was a mechanical engineer. Although tests indicate that he has a high IQ, Steven says that he was a poor student, and, in addition, he was overweight and not very popular.

When he was about eight years old, however, Steven found something that excited him and that he could call his own. As it turned out, Steven had a passion for work. There were mulberry trees in the Belmonte's back yard, and he would pick and package the fruit, then sell it door-to-door. He also picked flowers, made them into bouquets, wrapped them in newspaper, and sold them. He solicited neighbors for his snow-shoveling business and even created handwritten contracts for them to sign. In the summers he mowed lawns. And then, when he was twelve, he decided to go "big time." He went to his uncle, who was the Regional Director for the Fuller Brush Company, and became the youngest Fuller Brush man the company had ever had.

Every day after school, while the other kids were playing ball or doing their homework, he put on his little black suit jacket and adult-looking hat, stowed his sample case in his bike basket, and rode out to River Forest, an affluent community about three miles from where he lived. It was his goal to make $100 a day, on which he would earn a 40 percent commission. Sometimes it took an hour, sometimes three, and sometimes he made it in one stop. It turned out that little Steven was a very good salesman, and the women to whom he sold his goods loved the fact that he was just a kid. They'd laugh and say, "Oh, my goodness! Does your mother know you're doing this? Come in. Sit down." And then they'd go to get him something to drink while he was reaching for his catalogue. At the end of the day, he'd stop in a restaurant and treat himself to a meal. The next year, he hung up his bike and started taking taxis.

Back then, if you worked for Fuller Brush, you never actually met any of the other salespeople or the people you worked for. All transactions were done through the mail. But at the end of the year, there was a banquet for everyone in the region held in the ballroom of the Holiday Inn West, in Melrose Park. At the end of his first year selling, Steven attended the banquet. He remembers wandering around as the other guys, all of whom were adults, were talking among themselves and drinking. Since he was a kid, no one paid much attention to him, and he was too shy to approach anyone. But then it was time to give out awards, they called out his name and were surprised when a young boy appeared. They asked where his father was and Steve was confused. He told them his father only helped him deliver the product. The people were astonished when they realized it was Steven who won two awards that night, one for doing the second highest volume of business in the region, and the other for being the highest volume newcomer.

Much as he enjoyed the fruits of his labors as a Fuller Brush man, Steven knew early on that what he really loved was the hospitality industry. Every time he went on vacation with his family and they checked into a hotel or motel, he'd check out the room, the little bars of soap in the bathroom, and think it was the neatest thing in the world.

When he was just sixteen he got a job as a desk clerk at the O'Hare Concord Motor Inn in Rosemont, and within six months was promoted to front desk manager. Then, shortly after that, he saw an ad for a job as assistant manager at the Executive House, a major hotel in downtown Chicago. He applied, lying about his age, and was hired. So at the age of seventeen, Steven Belmonte was the assistant manager of a 500-plus-room hotel on Wacker Drive. And he did a great job!

The next year, when he was eighteen, he saw another ad in the Chicago Tribune. This one was for the job of general manager at the O'Hare Airport Holiday Inn. He remembers thinking that they'd never hire anyone as young as he was, so he grew a mustache, put on a three-piece suit, and told them he was twenty-six. He wasn't even old enough to order a drink at the bar, but he became the youngest general manager in Holiday Inn's history. He remained with Holiday Inn for about ten years and, as Steven puts it, "My work was my play and I couldn't wait to get up in the morning to go to work."

Meanwhile, he was making investments with a small, Arkansas-based firm called the Equity Group, and when Holiday Inn didn't renew his boss's franchise for the hotel, Steven contacted the Group. The principals flew to Chicago, Steven presented them with his vision for the hotel, and they bought it. Less than a year later, they resold it, making a million-dollar profit. At that point, Steven suggested that they go into the hotel business, and Equity Hotel Corporation was born.

Starting basically from nothing, within less than ten years the company grew to be one of the top ten management companies in the country. For Steven, life was great. He was married and living in Arlington Heights, an affluent suburb of Chicago, with a pool in his back yard. But suddenly he hit a wall. He felt he'd learned all he could in the business and, still in his thirties, began asking himself, "Is this all there is?"

That's when another great opportunity dropped into his lap—although Steven didn't see it that way at first. He was asked by the man who was buying the Ramada brand to join the company as President, but that meant moving to New Jersey, and Steven had never lived anywhere but Chicago. Eventually, however, his wife talked him into it, and Steven now says it's the best decision he ever made. When he started, there were 470 Ramada Inns, and when he resigned almost eleven years later, as the longest standing president of a national franchised hotel chain, there were more than 1,000.

In 2002 Steven returned to his entrepreneurial roots and, drawing on his more than 30 years of experience, launched Hospitality Solutions, LLC, a full-service, nationwide consultation firm specializing in lodging industry issues at the hotel and corporate level.

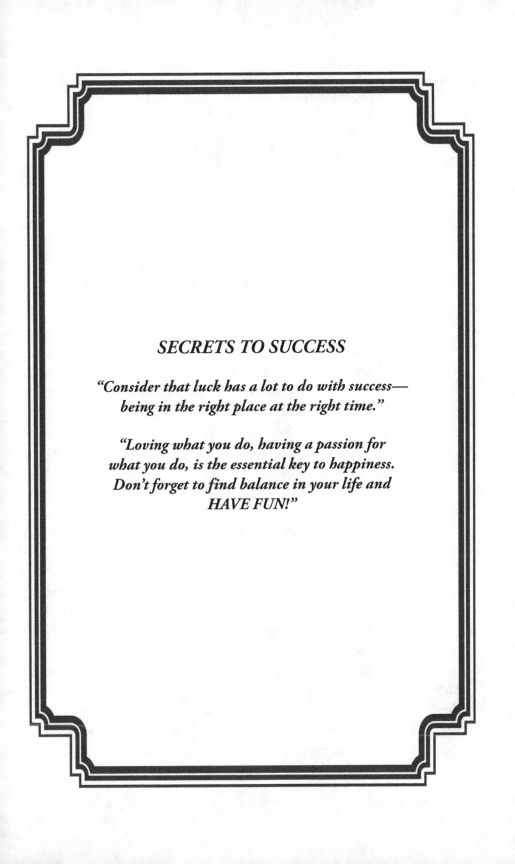

SECRETS TO SUCCESS

"Consider that luck has a lot to do with success—being in the right place at the right time."

"Loving what you do, having a passion for what you do, is the essential key to happiness. Don't forget to find balance in your life and HAVE FUN!"

Many years ago, I read an article about Mayor Flores that impressed me so much I cut it out and filed it away. Then, a couple of years later, when I began to write this book, I called her office and she agreed to a telephone interview. I have found her to be both strong and gracious, and I'm grateful for her participation. Mayor Flores has been married for 42 years and has raised two children. She also focuses much time on her grandson now.

LAREDO'S FIRST LADY

Elizabeth Flores

At 16, Elizabeth (Betty) Garcia met Antonio Flores, who, she found out later, had been carrying her picture in his wallet for three years before they met. The picture had appeared in Laredo's local newspaper when it was reported that Betty was the first girl to be elected ninth grade president. At the time, Antonio had declared to his mother that this was the girl he would marry, and they married one year after they met, when she was still a senior in high school.

Disappointed that their first-born would marry at such an early age and forego the college education they'd been sacrificing to save up for, Betty's parents nevertheless honored their eldest daughter's wishes. The consequence of that decision was that, although she was at the head of her class, Betty was asked to resign her leadership posts and give up her role as the lead in the school play. As a result, feeling let down and alone, she decided to quit school. She and her husband settled in Laredo, a dusty town whose biggest draw at the time was its proximity to the Mexican border.

Having made her choice, Betty was happy taking care of her husband and children. She came from a hard-working family and now she worked hard to be as good a wife and mother as she could possibly be. She knew her time would come, and when she later decided to enter the workforce, she chose a career in banking because it was a field where she felt she could make a difference. A successful banker for more than 29 years, she was the first female vice president in the bank's 100-year history. Betty retired in 1996 to work more closely with her community.

When she approached her husband about running to fill the term left unexpired when the mayor of Laredo, Saul Ramirez, was appointed HUD Secretary under President Clinton, she worried because they had promised to be supportive of one another's dreams – so long as those dreams did not involve political office. But when she asked, he answered, "You know, I have being thinking the same thing."

"That was when I knew I could win," Betty says. "Antonio and I have a different thought process, so having him come up with the same conclusion was phenomenal."

In 1998 Betty became Laredo's first woman mayor and was re-elected for another four-year term in 2002. Her first big project was the construction of Laredo's fourth international bridge. Plans for the bridge had been stalled for years, but when she and two other women took charge, it became a reality. The World Trade Bridge (which she also named) is an international crossing point for commercial goods only whose construction financing and continued success have become Laredo legend.

In addition to completing the bridge project, Betty also challenged the community to invest in building an entertainment center. The voters agreed to raise the sales tax by a quarter of a penny in order to build a premier multiuse arena that now draws top-notch entertainers and is home to one of the most successful ice hockey teams in the Central Hockey League, the Laredo Bucks.

When Mayor Flores was growing up in Laredo, its population was barely 50,000. Today, with 200,000 residents, it is considered one of fastest growing cities in the United States. For the first time since records have been kept, the unemployment rate is single-digit and soon to be below the state average. Its diversity, culture, and charm are a testament to the work of the people of Laredo, and to Laredo's first woman mayor, Elizabeth Flores.

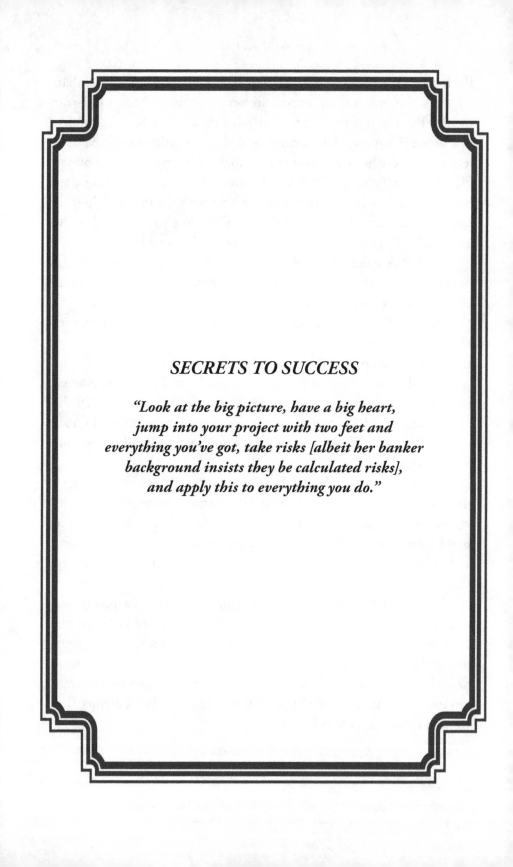

SECRETS TO SUCCESS

*"Look at the big picture, have a big heart,
jump into your project with two feet and
everything you've got, take risks [albeit her banker
background insists they be calculated risks],
and apply this to everything you do."*

I have a wonderful friend who, when he found out I was writing this book, announced, "I have the perfect person for your book," and gave me Joe Izzo's name. Now, Joe is an extremely busy guy, but he returned my phone call and we made an appointment. When I arrived at his shop, one of the first things I noticed was that it was so clean you could eat off the floors. He took the time to sit with me and answer my questions, and it turned out that he is one of the nicest people I have ever met. I can see why he's so successful. Joe has been married for seventeen years and has three children.

MAKE LEMONADE OUT OF LEMONS

Joe Izzo

Joe Izzo does his best to make lemonade out of lemons. In the 1960s, growing up with attention deficit disorder was a huge struggle. At the time, few educators were even aware of ADD and kids who had it were most often just thought of as lazy. Because of his disability, Joe had difficulty keeping up in school, and after years of teachers' pushing him through to the next grade, he finally gave up and just stopped going. "Finally at sixteen," he says, "my father said to me, 'You're wasting time and the taxpayers' money. Get a job!' " So his father signed him out of school and Joe got a job.

But many people who have a deficiency in one area seem to excel in another, and Joe was no exception. He found a job painting motorcycles, discovered he had an innate artistic ability, and began to develop a passion for automotive painting. "Being able to recreate and enhance the factory finish after it had been destroyed was very rewarding and fulfilling," explains Joe.

Gradually, he began to set his sights on more high-end cars, and a friend of his brother arranged for him to be taken on as a body painter at a Cadillac dealership. As the customers got to know him personally, he soon developed his own clientele. In the early 80s, he took a crack at establishing his own body painting business, but he was young, with no business experience, and it ultimately folded by the end of the decade.

Joe knew that if he wanted to be successful, he needed to become more business savvy. As fate would have it, he stumbled upon a brochure advertising a three-day seminar on how to be a successful business owner that was to be sponsored by the 3M Corporation. "It dramatically turned my focus around," says Joe. "It made a big difference, and I began to seek out different kinds of seminars related to my industry to help me grow my business."

He also began working with an older man who took him under his wing and treated him like a son. Joe listened and learned from his mentor whose philosophy for success was, "If you don't own the building you work in, then you are not in business."

Having heard that advice many times before, Joe knew he'd have to take a chance. In the end, he befriended a gentleman who knew of a building for sale. It felt right to Joe, so he took the plunge, and he still owns that building today. "It was 5,000 square feet and the first day I walked in there," Joe says, "I asked myself what I was going to do with all that space, but within six or seven years it was barely large enough to accommodate my business."

It was time to look for a bigger place. There was a 17,000-square-foot building right behind his, but the owner had already accepted a bid from someone else. Joe offered more and got the space, which is now home to his business, J & B Body Works, a full-service body shop that restores vehicles.

He was getting used to setting lofty goals, and his three-family house felt like it was getting smaller, too, so in about 1995, keeping the house as an investment, Joe purchased property to build a larger home, where his family now lives. As a result, he is now the owner of four properties.

Lately, Joe's lemonade is sparkling. He has turned his ADD into something positive. His body shop, which specializes in high-end cars like Ferraris, Mercedes Benz, and BMWs, employs a crew of finely trained technicians. "Because of my ADD and lack of education, I was smart enough to figure out early on that I wasn't able to apply the knowledge from the seminars without help," said Joe. "I hired capable people who are able to do what I can't do, but I wouldn't give up my ADD for anything. It gives me the ability to keep10 balls in the air at one time."

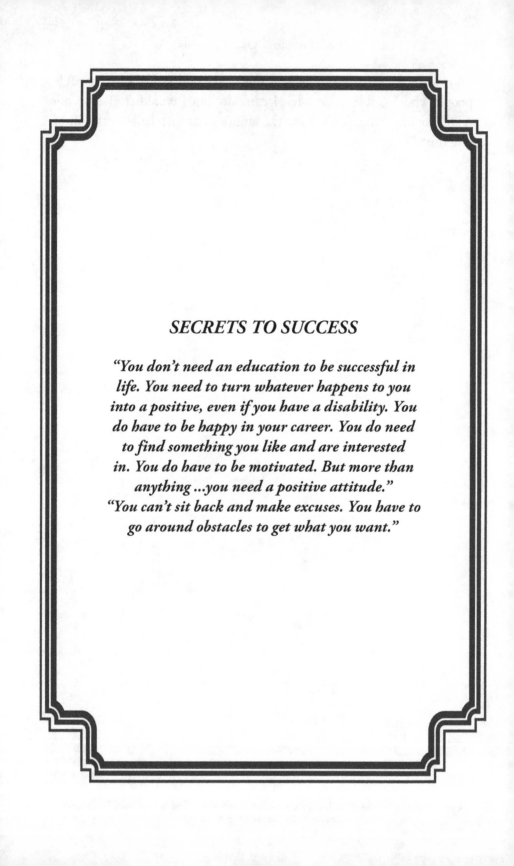

SECRETS TO SUCCESS

"You don't need an education to be successful in life. You need to turn whatever happens to you into a positive, even if you have a disability. You do have to be happy in your career. You do need to find something you like and are interested in. You do have to be motivated. But more than anything …you need a positive attitude."
"You can't sit back and make excuses. You have to go around obstacles to get what you want."

Maureen and I have been friends for a long time. We attended the same seminar many years ago, and I noticed her because she kept popping up to share. I knew I wanted to meet her, so, at the end of the weekend I introduced myself. We became close friends and have spent many vacations together skiing and lying in the sun. I value her friendship, her tremendous wisdom, and the help she's given me on various projects, including this book.

CULTIVATE YOUR TALENTS FOR SUCCESS

Maureen Chatfield

Maureen Chatfield lives in a magnificent, sprawling 10,000-square-foot home set on a New Jersey hilltop, which she shares with her partner, Donald, her college-age son, Alex, from a previous marriage, and her two adorable Jack Russell terriers, Nelly and Zoe. Her older son, Nick, is a recent Tish Film School graduate and lives in Manhattan.

An only child, Maureen remembers, as a little girl, feeling dearly loved by both her gentle mother and her dashing, playful father. When she was very young, he would carry her on his shoulders and have endearing conversations with her. "Who loves you the most?" he would ask, and she would giggle, "You do." "How do you know?" "Because you just told me so," she'd reply. It was their ritual.

Before long, however, it became evident that her home was not a safe place to be. Her father, an engineer with Grumman Aviation, lost his job, then another and another. Alcohol had made him violent and abusive. On an almost nightly basis there would be fights that ended up in Maureen's room with her mother looking for safety. It got to the point where she was terrified he would kill her mother and she'd be left alone with him.

On one occasion when she was just five years old, she remembers being in the bathroom with her father as he was combing his hair. He said something to her (she doesn't remember what), and her automatic childish response for some reason sent him into a rage. All of a sudden, he grabbed the hairbrush and smashed it over her head. It was at that moment she knew absolutely that she could never trust him again, ever.

When she was thirteen, Maureen moved out of her parents' house for the first time and went to live with a friend up the block. Her mother had actually thrown her father out of the house at that point and got a restraining order to prevent him from returning. He was gone for a whole summer, but then, slowly but surely, he began manipulating his way back, promising to fix things around the house, taking her mother out to dinner, buying her presents. After a year, her mother let him back in the house, and the nightmare returned.

Despite her family problems, however, Maureen was a brilliant student who was elected to the National Honor Society and won regional awards for her art. But life became so painful that she developed colitis and a sleep disorder. On the verge of a nervous breakdown, she left home and moved in with a girlfriend's family. Her dream of becoming an art teacher dissolved when she realized that path wouldn't create enough money to distance herself from her unhappy roots. She dropped out of high school in her senior year without graduating, and, although she later got her GED, she missed her prom and all the fun of senior year.

All she knew was that she had to get away from her father. He wouldn't let her go to college away from home, and living under his roof wasn't an option. He'd never encouraged her to pursue college because "smart women" were aggressive and unappealing and, in any case, he had already squandered all her college money.

At that point, Maureen was spending as much time as she could at her friend Angela's house. Angela came from a large, loving Italian family. In fact, she had everything Maureen wanted: a happy, peaceful family, a great boyfriend, and a new car. Angela wasn't a particularly great student and was going to hairdressing school. Maureen saw her way out. She knew there was a fair amount of money to be made in the beauty business, so she went to hairdressing school and was very good at it, all the while saying to herself, " I am going to make a lot of money." She knew she wanted to be an entrepreneur. By her own admission, she always had big dreams and big ambitions and the thought of having a predictable, moderate income seemed like a prison sentence.

She began to work passionately as a hairdresser in a salon on 57th Street in New York City, where her charismatic personality and hair cutting artistry quickly brought her success. Soon she had her own salon with six employees on an upper floor on Madison Avenue and 64th Street. And, although she was not aware of it at the time, she was also a visionary. There was a ground floor salon across the street, and every day on her way to work she would cheerfully pat the window and say like a mantra, "I want this space for my business. This space is coming to me." This went on for about a year until one day the owner of that salon called out of the blue to ask if she wanted to go into partnership with him.

After bringing in the lion's share of the business (now ten operators to his two), she was eventually able to take over the entire salon. There she attracted a celebrity roster of clients with limousines lined up out front, including Joe Namath, Freddy Prince, Rupert Murdock, and Roy Cohn, among others. She was praised by James Alexander of the New York Times as one of the five best hairsculpters in the country. And Vogue magazine had written about her talents as well. It was, in fact, the article in Vogue that brought her first husband, Bradley, into the salon. A successful architect working for I. M. Pei, Bradley introduced her to his great circle of friends, all of them highly and formally educated. It was then Maureen realized that even though she was making more money than many of them, she didn't really feel good about herself. She thought she needed to complete her education. At one point she even enrolled in Hunter College, then left to study acting at HB Studios, then moved on to FIT to study fashion. She had thought a college degree would dispel her "less than" feeling, but the experience wasn't strong enough to compel her to stay.

She and Brad were divorced, and then she met Kim, a Harvard Porcellian man who had also come into her salon. They fell in love and had a whirlwind courtship followed by a storybook wedding in Barbuda. Maureen and Kim were married for ten years and had two wonderful sons. In 1980 they opened a restaurant called Chatfield's on the Upper

East Side of Manhattan where Dina Merrill and Cliff Robertson, Paul Newman and Joanne Woodward, novelists Kurt Vonnegut and John Irving, Jim Henson, creator of the Muppets, and financier Don Marron were regulars.

However, despite a three-page article at the center of New York magazine and being on the Women's Wear Daily "In" list for seven years, they wanted to raise their children in the country. They decided to close the restaurant and move to New Jersey, where they opened another Chatfield's. Kim ran the restaurant and Maureen began to paint. Eventually, the marriage ran into difficulties, and she and Kim decided to separate. But Maureen continued to paint. She was offered a show in a Paris gallery and was selling fairly steadily, but didn't have enough work completed.

Several years later she had a very successful show at a gallery at the Riverside Studio gallery in New Jersey, where fourteen of her paintings sold on opening night. She received many local awards and then a national award from American Artists magazine in 1995. Her works have become part of the Merk, Lawford/Kennedy, Hapsburg, Washburn, and Britton collections.

Always a woman of many talents, after she and Kim divorced, Maureen used her ingenuity to create an extremely successful and exclusive introduction company, through which she met her current and long-term partner. Donald came in as a client and ended up inviting her to his ski house for the weekend. On the five-hour drive up to the mountain, it was clear that they were really clicking, and when they stopped at Dunkin' Donuts, he turned to her and asked, "So, should I ask you to marry me right now or wait a while?"

Two years before she met Donald, Maureen had a clear vision of the house she was going to live in. She wrote in her journal that it was stucco, Georgian, large and sunny, with a big heated swimming pool. There would be a great painting studio off the main living area that would have a stone fireplace and large, old beams across the ceiling. The basement would have a pool table, TV, stereo, and dart board. That's the home she wound up building and decorating with Donald a decade later.

Maureen still runs her introduction company, teaches art in her studio on Tuesdays, and is working with New York galleries to build her painting clientele. Now she says, "I can finally say that I like who I am, I'm really okay."

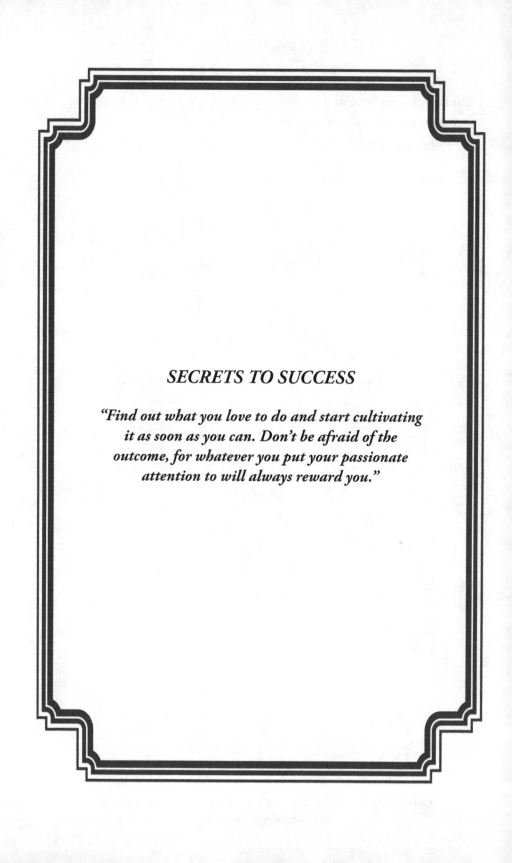

SECRETS TO SUCCESS

"Find out what you love to do and start cultivating it as soon as you can. Don't be afraid of the outcome, for whatever you put your passionate attention to will always reward you."

I met Catherine through a friend who raved about her and said that I absolutely must meet her. When I drove up to "Apple Hill," we met in her office, which is decorated with trophies, awards, and informal photos of her family. By the time the interview was over, I knew exactly why my friend had been so insistent that we get together. Catherine has been married for over thirty years and has two lovely daughters.

FEAR CAN MOTIVATE

Catherine Del Spina

Warm, bright, and sophisticated, Catherine Del Spina lives with her husband of twenty-four years, two teenage daughters, a housekeeper, and their two boxer dogs, Bert and Ernie, in a graceful, renovated old house on a hilltop overlooking a reservoir about an hour and a half from New York City. The landscaped grounds of "Apple Hill," as the property is named, are surrounded by a stone wall and include apple, Asian pear, plum, and peach trees, as well as bocce and tennis courts and a swimming pool.

From a cottage office on the grounds, Catherine runs a $40 million wholesale business devoted to designer household specialty items that sell to Bed, Bath and Beyond, Linens 'n Things, and other similar retail outlets. But, life for Catherine was not always so luxurious.

"Our family began to break up when I was fourteen," she says. "Before that, we lived in a nice house in New Jersey, and just after I finished eighth grade we moved to a new development in Florida. My oldest brother was already working in New York, my middle brother was in high school, and my younger brother was five at the time.

"One day my mother just announced that she was taking my youngest brother, Thomas, and moving back to New Jersey to care for her ailing father. My middle brother, Bud, and I stayed in Florida with my father. It was devastating for me, and I found out that my parents were getting divorced by reading about it in the newspaper."

After a while, her mother returned to Florida and moved into the house where Catherine and Bud were living with their father. But things didn't get any better; in fact they got worse. They couldn't pay the rent, the water, heat, and electricity were shut off, and they received an eviction notice. At that point, Catherine's father left for good, and Bud sold his college books for food. Their mother had a nervous breakdown and was taken away in an ambulance. When she returned, they moved into a trailer.

"I moved three times during that period, but it was all so confusing that it's difficult for me to remember where and for how long.

"My mother took the first job she'd ever had in her life, working as a clerk in a small discount clothing store. Because we'd lost our cars, my brother had to drive her to work on his motor scooter, and I just remember thinking how pathetic it was that, at the age of forty-something, she was riding on the back of a scooter for transportation.

"We had no idea where my father was—no telephone number and no financial support. Then, in the early seventies, he was indicted in the state of New Jersey for misappropriating funds from the company where he'd worked in the sixties. Although he said he was falsely accused, he was sent to prison for a few years. I remember taking a bus and a train to visit him. That was a very scary time for me.

"While I was still in Florida I took my SATs and was accepted at the University of Florida, but shortly after that I moved back to New York to live with my older brother, Don, who had become like a surrogate father to me. I thought about going to college in the city, but that wasn't my idea of what college campus life should be, and, in any case, I had to support myself.

Don had gone to college and so had my father, but even so, Dad used to make fun of Don, calling him "Joe College." Bud went to junior college, but my mother hadn't gone at all, and I got the impression that it wasn't something my father admired.

I don't remember anyone in my family even suggesting that I should go to college. For a long time it was so humiliating to me that I kept it a deep, dark secret. I remember that when I had to tell my children, who think of college as just a natural part of life, they didn't believe me at first. In fact, one of the things that initially drew me to my husband was his intellect and education.

But, as I said, I didn't go; I went to work instead. One of my first jobs was waiting tables, and while I was doing that I just naturally expanded the job by promoting parties at the restaurant, which, of course, brought in more business. That made me feel so good about myself that I applied for a job at the Pottery Barn. My boss there turned out to be a wonderful mentor. He was a Maine gentleman who wore corduroy jackets, khaki pants, and loafers, and he didn't care that I was twenty-one years old, with no college education and no business experience beyond waiting tables. He saw that I had potential, and his belief in me made me feel more and more confident.

"After about a year and a half, I'd developed contacts of my own; people in the industry began to know who I was, and I decided to start my own business. That was twenty-five years ago, and I now feel that I've done all I want to with this enterprise and am looking into the sale of the business. My goals have changed and I want to spend some time giving back to the community in whatever way I can—through leadership, or lectures, or charity."

Catherine says that, since the time she was almost homeless as a teenager, the theme of her inner voice has been, "No, not me. I never want to be caught in a position like that again." Her business and the security of her marriage have allowed her to provide her daughters with a childhood experience that is very different from her own.

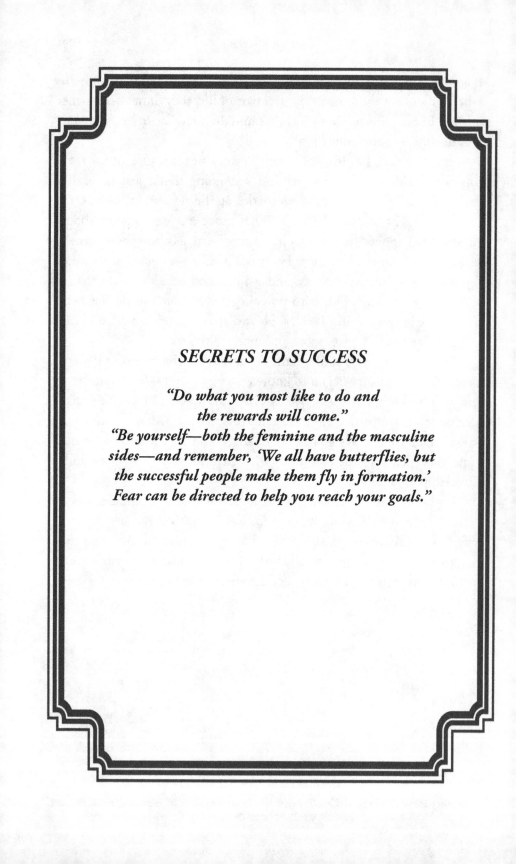

SECRETS TO SUCCESS

*"Do what you most like to do and
the rewards will come."*
*"Be yourself—both the feminine and the masculine
sides—and remember, 'We all have butterflies, but
the successful people make them fly in formation.'
Fear can be directed to help you reach your goals."*

I met Len and Caren by chance one day when my son asked me to go to a memorabilia store to look for a comic book. We looked through the Yellow Pages and found The Joker's Child, which turned out to be a wonderful place. When I began writing this book, I knew that I wanted them to be a part of it. Len and Caren have been married for nineteen years.

COMICS ARE SERIOUS BUSINESS

Len and Caren Katz

Len and Caren Katz are the proprietors of The Joker's Child, a 2,600¬square-foot comic book shop in Fair Lawn, New Jersey. They have owned the store for seventeen years. You might say that it's a business Caren married along with her husband. She has an accounting background and handles the numbers end.

Born in the Bronx, Len spent most of his childhood in Queens, New York, the child of Polish/Jewish parents who had lived for some time in Israel, where his older brother and sister were born. Although his brother did spend some time in college, his sister never attended, and his parents never pushed college for him. Possibly because he was ten years younger than his older brother—a kind of afterthought, Len says—and his parents both worked, they mostly just let him alone so long as he didn't get in trouble. He also thinks they realized that if they tried to make any rules to restrict him, he'd just design ways to get around them, and Len thinks that was a pretty good thing because it gave him the freedom to figure out what he really wanted to do.

When he was eighteen, they even moved to Florida. Len goes to visit them, but he says he gets "itchy" if he's too far away from New York for too long.

He didn't do badly in school, but it wasn't a priority either, and he actually finished his last year of high school at the Quintanos School for Young Professionals in Manhattan, where many of his classmates were working in the theater. "There were several tests we had to pass to graduate, but we literally didn't have to be at school most of the time. That was my favorite year in high school ever."

Collecting comics has been his hobby since he was ten, at about the same time he got his first job, which was working in a card shop putting together the weekend editions of the New York Times and the Daily News. He says it's the worst job he's ever had but he liked it anyway because the store also sold comic books. After that, he more or less went into business for himself, running his first Star Trek convention and selling his first comics when he was just thirteen. Len says he "just fell into it" because he and his friends were all involved with Star Trek. And even now he still loves comics.

Before opening the comic book store, however, Len worked at J & R Music World, a large electronics store near City Hall in Manhattan. After that, he moved to another store in midtown, where he thought the opportunities would be better. But it didn't work out, and when he was let go, his unemployment checks gave him the time to decide what to do next. That's how The Joker's Child was born. Caren had to leave her own job within six months because Len couldn't handle the store without her.

He and Caren had a little money saved from wedding presents and absolutely no debt—"Caren is phobic about debt," Len says. "Anything that creates debt is something she wants to get rid of very quickly"—so they started scouting locations in New Jersey, looking for schools and monitoring traffic patterns—and opened their first shop in Fair Lawn (they've moved only once since, when they needed more space) because it was located in the midst of five high schools and a grade school.

Len donated his collection, although he didn't really think he had that many comic books, and the shop quickly became successful. This was 1988; in 1989 the "Batman" movie opened and suddenly everyone wanted Batman "stuff." Comic book stores were the place to go, and The Joker's Child had a lot of Batman paraphernalia.

"There's a new craze every five or ten years," Len says. When they moved to their new location in 1996, it was Pokemon. "There were lines snaking through the store; it was crazy." But even between crazes, comics are an evergreen business. About six hundred new titles are issued each month, and customers regularly spend anywhere from five to fifty dollars a week.

Len and Caren have never had children, although through the store they have had many. They're okay with that because, as Len says, "Most people say that when they're older they can't wait to have grandchildren, but the truth is, when I'm older I just want to be able to sleep. The one thing I've learned is that when you're in the retail business, your free time is worth more than gold."

A few years ago, he and Caren actually started closing the shop for vacation one week a year, which, according to Len, in the comic book business is insane. "Comic book collectors, real comic book collectors, have to have their books on a weekly basis. Imagine if you watched a particular soap opera, and then the network tells you, 'Well, you're not getting your soap opera next week, but you can get it from somebody else.' It's the same thing with comics." But they've decided that no matter what it costs them in business, they need that one week a year; otherwise they'd go insane. Sometimes they even take a weekend, which causes some distress among their clientele, but they manage.

They now have a website, but so far it only gives directions and shows photos of the brick and mortar store. Len does realize, however, that when you sell via the Internet, you don't physically have to be in the shop and you can expand your clientele exponentially, so he and Caren are now looking to sell online and make it profitable.

Despite the hard work and occasional grumbling, Len says they're happy with what they've achieved.

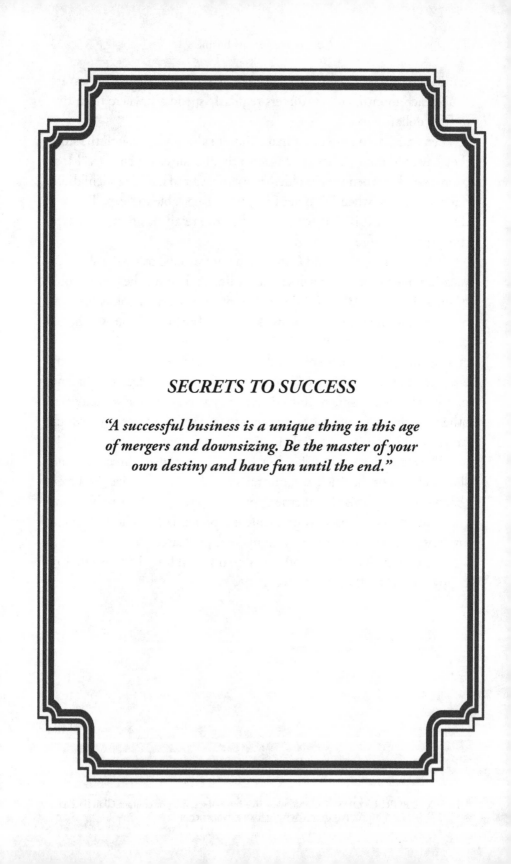

SECRETS TO SUCCESS

"A successful business is a unique thing in this age of mergers and downsizing. Be the master of your own destiny and have fun until the end."

Liz came to me serendipitously through an acquaintance who heard I was writing this book. *Although I was well aware of her accomplishments,* when we met at a quaint little café house near her *home in New York City, I was most impressed by her warmth, her vibrant youthfulness, and her apparent lack of ego. I'm grateful to have had the opportunity to meet her. Liz was married to Rick Derringer for 22 years.*

CONTACTS ARE KEY TO GETTING AHEAD

Liz Derringer

A delightful woman with a peaches-and-cream complexion, Liz Derringer's unassuming demeanor belies her drive and ambition. A native New Yorker, she is the head of her own public relations firm and divides her time between New York City and Southampton, on Long Island.

Derringer and Weitz Communications work with top-selling artists including Thomas Kinkade and Peter Max, as well as high-profile organizations like the Muscular Dystrophy Foundation, and events such as the Super Bowl, the Grammy Awards, the World Series, the U.S. Tennis Open, and both the Republican and Democratic National Conventions. Despite all her success, however, Liz admits to having overcome many insecurities, which she now attributes to the lack of structure in her household while she was growing up in Greenwich Village.

Her mother, a divorcee, spent most of her time pursuing a successful career in the cosmetics industry and working with Charles Revson of Revlon, as well as Helena Rubenstein, and Polly Bergen. Neither her mother nor her father, who worked in the garment industry, are college graduates, and although both her older sister and younger brother did attend college, Liz says that there was very little conversation about higher education in her family, and she herself "barely graduated high school."

With her mother working much of the time and her father out of the home, there was no one paying much attention to what she, the middle child, was doing. Left to her own devices, she remembers, at the age of fifteen, watching the television show "Shindig" and seeing the then-budding young rock star Rick Derringer. Liz says that the moment she saw him, she knew Rick was the man she would marry, so she made it her business to find out where his next gig would be and went to the hotel to wait for him.

Since no one in her family ever asked, "Do you know where your children are?" Liz began traveling with Rick, going from city to city as he pursued his career, picking up her own "street wise" education along the way and preparing for her own career— although she didn't know it at the time. After three years, they were married.

The Derringers' travels brought them in contact with some of the biggest names in the music world, including the legendary record producer Clive Davis, and performers Aerosmith, Led Zeppelin, and Cindy Lauper, as well as Meatloaf, Steely Dan, and Barbra Streisand— and because she both loved and believed in him, Liz did whatever she could to promote Rick.

Along the way, she forged a relationship with Andy Warhol, who, when he started Interview, dubbed her "Mrs. Rock," and asked her to interview rock stars for the magazine. Her first interview was with Elton John's lyricist and songwriter, Bernie Taupan, and interviews with Mick Jagger, Rod Stewart, Stevie Nicks, and Sting soon followed. At that point, Liz still thought of her work as a hobby rather than a career, but she knew that she needed something of her own to build her self-esteem and provide what she felt was missing from her life.

Despite her less-than-stellar high school career, Liz has a great love of learning and took it upon herself to continue her self-education by studying writing, acting, singing, dance, literature, history, and French. Although she was still insecure, she remembered that her writing teacher had told her she had a special talent, and that became the direction she pursued. She went on to become a columnist for the New York Daily News and wrote for magazines including Playboy and Harper's Bazaar.

In the course of her career she met Frank Radice, who was at that time a producer for CNN Entertainment. A musician himself, Radice went to see Rick perform and Liz begged her husband to let him come up on stage. Frank was thrilled, and her association with him gave her the break she needed. After she sent him tapes of interviews she'd done with Julian Lennon, John Taylor, and Duran Duran, he hired her for CNN as a producer/reporter.

At about this time, Rick had a gig playing with the cover girl and singer Rosie Vela, who was Peter Max's girlfriend. As it turned out, Max's assistant had left and he was desperately in need of someone to handle his scheduling and appointments. Rosie encouraged Liz to take the job, and she wound up becoming not Peter's assistant, but his public relations director—a position she held for more than thirteen years. Working with him gave her some remarkable experiences, including lunch with Prince Rainier of Monaco and an opportunity to meet President Ronald Reagan. After 23 years, however, Liz and Rick's marriage was falling apart. She was devastated. Having been with him since she was a teenager, she couldn't imagine what she would do without him, and for a while, she says, she almost had a nervous breakdown. In fact, the only thing that kept her going was her work with Peter Max. But after the divorce, she pulled herself together and started Derringer & Weitz Commmunications with Michael Weitz, whom she'd met through Peter Max, and who represented the French artist Michael Delacroix.

At this point Liz is remarried and her life has, in a way, come full circle as she is now representing the young rock 'n roll singer/songwriter Dominick. Although she's had to call upon the people she'd met over the years in the music business, she's always kept up those relationships and enjoyed their friendship.

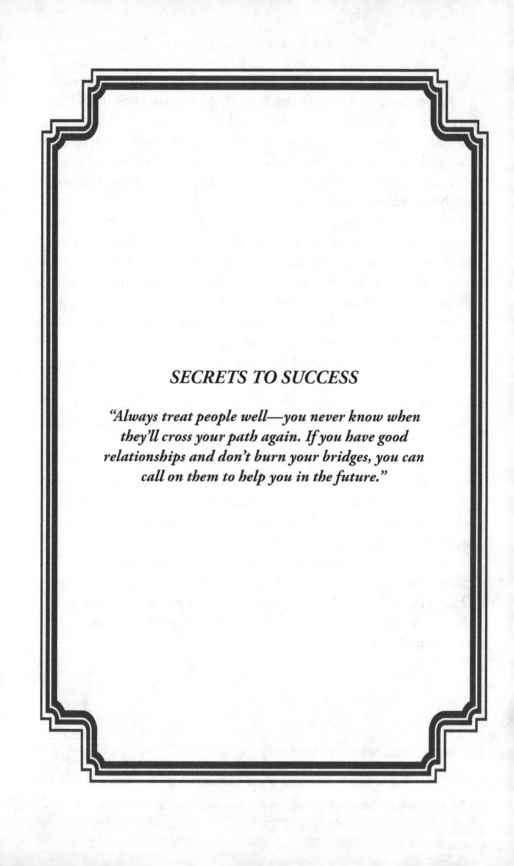

SECRETS TO SUCCESS

*"Always treat people well—you never know when
they'll cross your path again. If you have good
relationships and don't burn your bridges, you can
call on them to help you in the future."*

When I chose to leave my apartment for three months, I needed to find someone I could trust to take care of my two cats, Acorn and Blackjack. As luck would have it, I met a woman at a conference I was attending who turned out to be a real animal lover. She not only took care of my cats, but when I told her about my book project, she exclaimed, "My Uncle Fenton would fit right into your book! He's a self-made entrepreneur." When I called Fenton, he was very open to doing the interview, and as I talked with him, I realized he was a highly motivated individual with a very generous heart. Fenton has been married for 20 years and has one son and two daughters.

CREATE YOUR OWN LUCK

Fenton Soliz

When Fenton Soliz was 15, he longed to buy a boat. He had his eye on a particular model—a 12-foot fiberglass fishing boat he'd seen at Sears. Fenton was determined to have it. Working every summer at his parent's hotel on Cape Cod, Massachusetts, he was serious about saving money and even made a special "money box" out of an old container. On the cover he wrote "Do Not Touch."

And he didn't touch that money until it was time to buy the boat. One Saturday morning, Fenton and his father, who was a successful dentist in Westchester County, New York, took him to Sears. Fenton stood back admiring the purchase he was about to make. He could hardly contain his excitement—he would be a motorboat owner before he could even drive a car! "I said to my father, 'Well, here's the boat! Now we have to go over to the motors.' " Fenton naturally assumed that his father would pay for the motor. Instead, his father showed him a nice pair of oars. It was a lesson he never forgot. He learned to work hard for what he wanted. "When I look back at the motivation for my hard work," he says, "it was clearly my parents, because hard work is all we knew as a family. My parents gave us an incredible foundation with a lot of balance."

To order DEGREES OF SUCCESS, view live interviews, blog or contact Claudia Fox: Go to www.thefoxwayworks.com

Now 45 years old, Fenton grew up in the 70s, the era of tie-dye, hippy hair, and Led Zeppelin, and with his full, bushy Afro, he looked the part. He was an average B or C student, but what he lacked in academic motivation, he certainly made up for in spirit. Passionate about sports, he played on his high school football and baseball teams and was involved in all sorts of extracurricular activities, serving as president of the Ecology Club and president of the Future Business Leaders of America. In fact, he was so popular with such a diverse group of people that he was the second most photographed person in his yearbook.

Although his family believed strongly in higher education and assumed that Fenton would attend college as his siblings did, he never did become passionate about academics. After floundering in and out of a local community college and even trying his hand at a technical institute, he realized that nothing was coming together for him and started to question his reasons for going to school—was he doing it for himself, or for his family?

After taking some time to think about it, he realized he was searching for something else: the sense of belonging that comes from being in a group but doesn't require taking exams. Fenton was looking for a community and found it, accidentally, in theater. "My older brother was in a theater group—an off-off-Broadway play, and he asked me to be one of the understudies. It was very exciting and sophisticated," he recalls. "I never actually went on but the sense of belonging I felt gave me an incredible confidence that I could do anything I set my mind to. And I thought, 'I can do that. I can do that!' "

No idea was too small for Fenton, so when it came time to step out into the real world, he found a job working as a secretary for a real estate management company. That typing class he took in high school to be closer to the girls turned out to be a real plus! Fenton worked hard and earned the respect of his supervisor, who gave him more and more responsibility. He didn't mind learning from the bottom up and began to emulate the executives around him. He learned to walk the walk and talk the talk. And he got noticed.

Ultimately, he rose through the ranks to manage the firm's five high-end office buildings in White Plains. As the liaison between the tenants and management, Fenton became the "face" of the management office.

One day, two men calling themselves mortgage brokers rented space in the building where he worked. On the advice of his father, who owned some rental properties, Fenton had already gotten a real estate license, so when these two entrepreneurs asked him to join their fledgling company a few months later, he decided to make the leap. At first he knew nothing about the mortgage business, which, at the time, was totally unregulated, but he quickly went from being in the middle of a deal and not even knowing what mortgage points were to becoming one of the company's top sellers. "I was getting mortgages in buildings like Trump Tower and it was great," says Fenton.

When he decided to go out on his own, the decision seemed like a no-brainer. Everything was coming together: he had the ambition, the drive, and the passion. In the beginning, he worked out of his apartment in White Plains, which was directly across the street from his old company. Then, when his co-op management disapproved, he bought a two-family house and moved his business operations there. "Those were the fabulous years, and we couldn't do anything wrong," he says. "Then came 1989 and the start of a real downturn in the economy. For the first time, IBM laid off employees. No one was refinancing. I had 35 people working for me and didn't even know how I was going to make payroll."

Deals that usually took six months to complete were now taking twelve. Banks were not approving mortgages. Fenton began to wonder how he was going to turn his business around. He had a family by then, and he really needed to take a good look at his life. He began reading self-help books and attended seminars. "I wasn't sure how I was going to get out of it, but I just kept showing up every day, and somehow we all got through it. I worked seven days a week and made cold calls until something happened." And eventually something did. The economy turned around, things got better, and Fenton's perseverance paid off.

His company has more than survived, and this year marks its 19th year. It is licensed in five states: New Jersey, New York, Connecticut, Massachusetts and Florida, and is thriving. "We've changed the way we've done business, going after more corporate accounts and aligning ourselves with another market," says Fenton. "I feel like I am a thoroughbred in this industry right now. I've had an opportunity to gallop in the best events and there is literally no one I would be apprehensive about going up against. Clients feel my passion, they can see it, and it makes a huge difference. I still feel like I am ready for anything."

Lately, he says, he's been feeling bored and is looking to kick it up a notch. "I want to go to another level, but I'm not sure what that looks like." No doubt he'll find out!

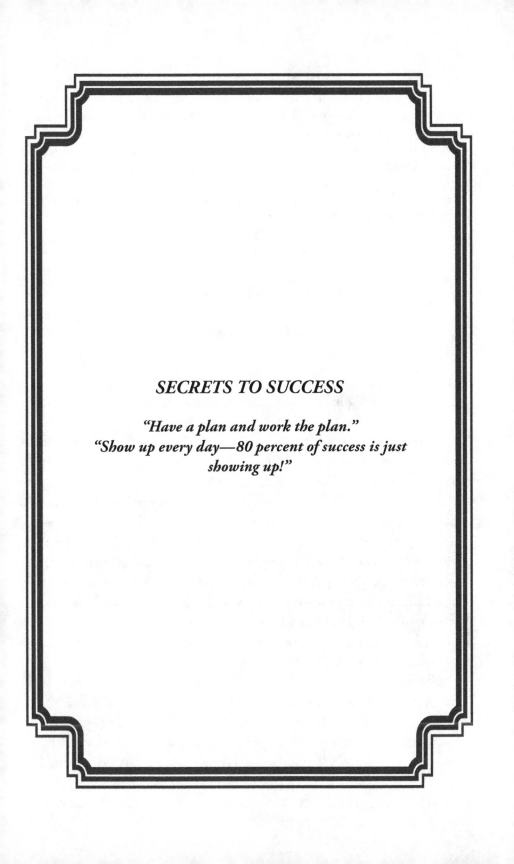

SECRETS TO SUCCESS

"Have a plan and work the plan."
*"Show up every day—80 percent of success is just
showing up!"*

When I first moved to New Jersey, I asked friends to recommend a colorist for my hair. I was a bit worried about giving up the salon I'd been going to in Manhattan, but one of my friends raved about JoAnn, so I decided to give her a try. When I arrived for my first appointment, I was greeted by a petite, smiling blonde. She was so friendly that I was immediately put at ease. Then, as she started the color process, it became very clear to me that she knew exactly what she was doing. That was sixteen years ago, and today I still go to her shop, although now my appointments are with Diane, one of the many operators she has trained.

COLOR MY WORLD

JoAnn Feder

School never intrigued JoAnn Feder as much as socializing. Growing up in Fair Lawn, New Jersey, JoAnn was well liked and popular, but was only an average student. Nothing seemed to click for her academically, until one day she accompanied her boyfriend to the Bergen Community Technical School in Teaneck, New Jersey. She peeked into a hairdressing class and says that, "The minute I caught a glimpse of the beauty culture, I said to myself, 'This is where I want to be.' It felt like home."

Of course, the registration deadline had passed, but JoAnn didn't give up. She knew this was the right place for her. She found a neighbor who knew the principal of the school, and with a lot of luck and an equal amount of determination, she was admitted even though the class was totally filled. Four years later, she graduated at the top of her class and, after winning first prize in a hairdressing competition, was asked to join a salon in Tenafly, New Jersey.

But after three years, JoAnn was getting restless. She was ready to take a risk. With absolutely no credit but a plethora of persistence, she applied for a loan and bought out an existing salon in Fort Lee. At the time, however, she was a young and inexperienced entrepreneur, and was barely making a living. "I had no idea what I was doing, but I learned how to work hard. I sat behind the front desk and thought the business was just going to run itself."

Eventually, she sold the business to get married and start a family. But four years later, she was divorced and needed to return to work. At that point, she took a job as an office manager, thinking that it would be more prestigious than returning to the beauty business. But that elitist mentality was short-lived.

By that time, Vidal Sassoon had created an aura prestige in the field of hair styling in London and was just beginning to have an impact in America as well. JoAnn took notice and succumbed to her destiny and opened a new specialty salon in Englewood called the Colour Room. This time it felt right. "I had the stationery printed before I even had an address," says JoAnn. "It was just a fantasy, but I made it happen!"

By now, she knew the beauty business better and was more prepared. She had taken entrepreneurial courses that helped her learn how to create budgets and set and meet deadlines. Most important, however, she became aware of her own potential.

JoAnn ran The Colour Room successfully for nine years. No sooner did she sell it, she started looking for a new space. The second Colour Room, located in Cresskill, New Jersey, has been running for 13 years, employing 15 colorists/stylists and catering to an eclectic clientele ranging from one-year-olds coming to get their first haircuts to teens and moms looking for the latest celebrity style and grandmothers who have standing weekly appointments. "Even men come in for haircuts and color," says JoAnn, who makes sure her staff keeps up with the latest trends in color and style.

Having weathered many ups and down, JoAnn believes that the secret to her success is to hire smiles. "Everyone who works for me has a great personality and they smile at the clients. You can always train someone but if they are not charismatic people, it doesn't matter how talented they are, the clients will not be attracted to coming back."

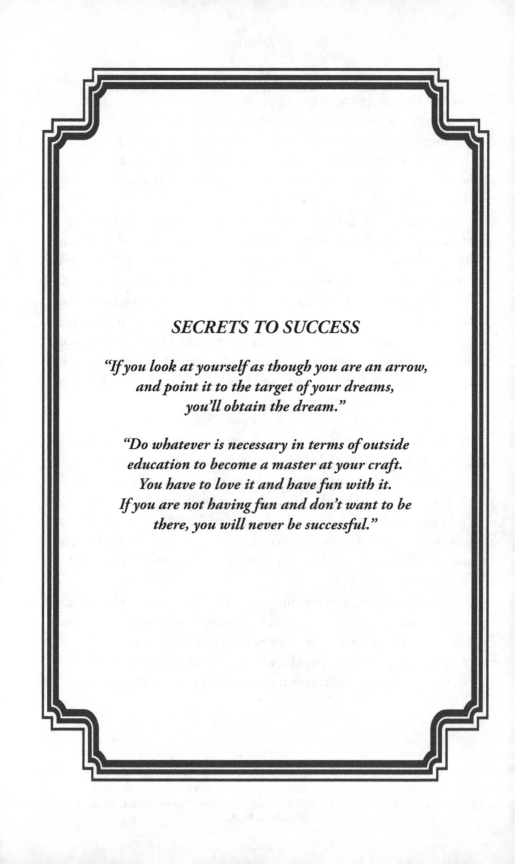

SECRETS TO SUCCESS

*"If you look at yourself as though you are an arrow,
and point it to the target of your dreams,
you'll obtain the dream."*

*"Do whatever is necessary in terms of outside
education to become a master at your craft.
You have to love it and have fun with it.
If you are not having fun and don't want to be
there, you will never be successful."*

Sean and I met when we both attended a barbecue at the home of a mutual friend. Afterwards, we went to visit her new home, and when I remarked on the silver-framed family photos displayed on the entrance table, she told me something about her family and the path she had taken to arrive where she is now. I'm delighted that she's been willing to share that story here.

RISK

Sean Hidey

Currently the Chief Administrative Officer for a hedge fund in Connecticut, Sean Hidey says that her career in finance really "found" her. Her first job in the field was at E. F. Hutton in Universal City, California, and she obtained it, as many people do their first jobs, through someone she knew, in this case through the mother of her then-current boyfriend.

Sean grew up in California and describes herself as "a Valley girl, born and raised." Her mother was a showgirl and her father a musician, and their marriage was quite rocky. In fact, they were divorced when Sean was seven and her brother was eight years old. After that, her mother was, as Sean says, "running scared." There was always a level of fear—about being a single parent and making ends meet—bubbling beneath the surface of her life.

After the divorce, her mother bought a "four-plex"—a building with four apartment units—and, by the time she was fifteen, Sean and her brother were living alone in one of the units because their mother had remarried and they weren't getting along. But her brother had an unpredictable temper, and eventually Sean moved in with her father. That arrangement wasn't ideal either, however, because her father was in some ways very lenient and in others very controlling, and Sean never knew what to expect from one day to the next.

She was paying her father's household bills, and—she now thinks it was to get back at him for his controlling behavior (because she knows she could have simply asked for the money)—she began to charge things she wanted for herself, pay the bill, and then destroy the canceled check so he wouldn't find out. But eventually he did find out, and he was furious. "Essentially he said, 'That's it. You defied me. You hurt me. You have two weeks to get a job and two weeks to get out of the house.' So I did. I found a little place for myself, and I got the job at E. F. Hutton."

Sean had already started attending college by then, and she continued taking classes at night for about a year and a half. But working all day and going to school at night was very difficult, and, as she says, "With a year and a half under my belt, I stopped. I just couldn't see the point. So that was the end of college for me and at the same time the beginning of my life in the financial world."

Luckily, Sean's first boss turned out to be a wonderful mentor for her. "Basically, I had no skills. I didn't know shorthand and I could barely type. She was so patient and sweet with me. Because I adored her, I wanted to please her."

After about two and a half years, she moved on to Cantor Fitzgerald, which is where she earned her first broker's license and went to work in the trading room. Sean had just turned twenty-one (a requirement for taking the test), and, she says, very few women took it back then, particularly at such a young age. "Most of the people in the exam room were men," she says, "so that was a big accomplishment for me."

Following Cantor Fitzgerald, there was a short-lived job at a hedge fund. "That was the only time I've ever been fired," Sean recalls. "It was stunning. From that mishap I deduced that one can always be fired. Everyone can be replaced." Following that, there was a brief stint at Morgan Stanley, and then eight years at Drexel Burnham in Beverly Hills with Michael Milken, the junk bond king. Of Drexel she says, "It was very exciting work and very stressful. You have trading orders coming at you from a myriad of different people. I kept my head down and my nose to the grindstone. I'm not one who is very curious about what everyone else is doing unless I need to be, if it enhances my knowledge and enhances my job. In that charged environment, I learned that it was necessary for me to stand up for myself, even though it was difficult for me. I began learning the art of constructive confrontation."

Along the way, Sean married and had a baby, whom she tragically lost to SIDS at the age of two months. Of that time Sean says, "When I found her, my first two thoughts were 'I will survive this; my marriage will not.' This has become a core belief for me. I will survive, I will thrive, and I will figure out what I need to do to get the job done and move forward.

"After three and a half months I went back to work at Drexel, but I didn't want to be on the trading floor any more. They found me a spot on the legal team, and I really enjoyed the work and did a great job, too." Sean stayed on at Drexel after the bankruptcy as a member of the transition team. She was divorced by then, and after Drexel finally shut its doors, she decided to take some time off. When she was ready to reenter the job market, however, she discovered that it wasn't as easy as she'd thought. After a few false starts, she was offered an interview with a Boston firm. That got her thinking—"If you're willing to move to Boston, why not New York? There were personal issues, too, that compelled me to make some sort of change in my life, so I started to contact people I knew on the East coast."

So, at the age of forty, Sean wound up in New York on the high yield bond trading floor with the Canadian Imperial Bancorp of Commerce. This, in turn, led to her spending six months working in London—an experience that was both pressure-filled and exciting. "And now I'm with a start-up hedge fund, which was definitely a risky move. Luckily, it's a risk I'm able to take at this point in my life. With a mixture of hard work and tenacity, I've 'lucked into' a successful career path," she says, "but I'd likely advise young people today to get a college degree if that's at all possible. And if it's impossible, I'd coach them to dig deep and ascertain their strengths and the endeavors that make them feel good about themselves. Then I'd counsel them to determine how those attributes could be put to work for them in the business world. Next I'd say, 'Believe in yourself and your abilities.' Because, honestly, I don't think any of the courses that were available in college would have prepared me for what I'm doing right now."

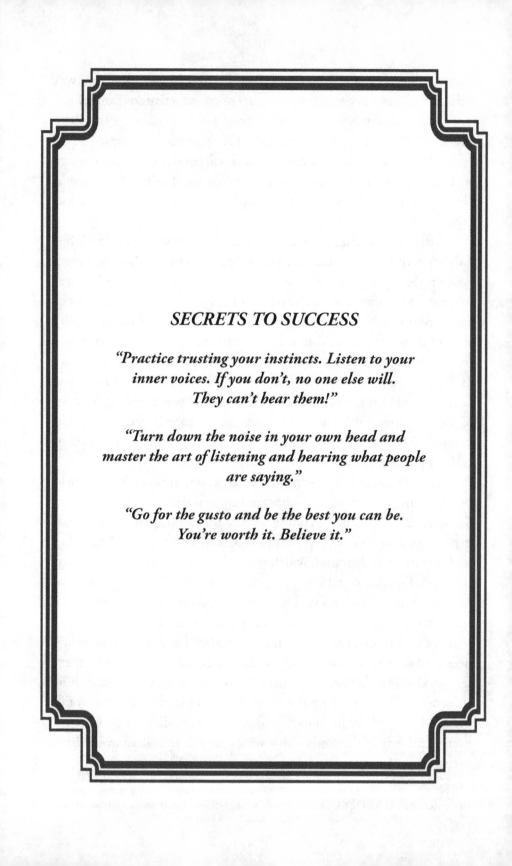

SECRETS TO SUCCESS

"Practice trusting your instincts. Listen to your inner voices. If you don't, no one else will. They can't hear them!"

"Turn down the noise in your own head and master the art of listening and hearing what people are saying."

"Go for the gusto and be the best you can be. You're worth it. Believe it."

Danny was the very first person that I interviewed for this book, so when I went to see him I was doubly nervous—first about how to conduct the interview process itself, and second, because I knew he was an extremely busy person. As it turned out, however, he's not only extremely busy, but also extremely thoughtful and accommodating. I'll never forget how he put me at ease and made sure I got all the information I needed. Danny is married and has two children.

TRUST YOUR INTUITION

Danny Goldberg

The Chairman and CEO of Artemis Records, Danny Goldberg remembers having had what he calls a "typical childhood" in New York City. Although he recalls being quite outgoing when he was a little kid, he became much more of an introvert as he grew up. Of his peers, he says, "There were the athletes and those who excelled academically, and I felt excluded from both." In the fall of 1965, however, he "discovered" rock 'n roll, embraced the sixties culture, and found the identity that worked for him.

Although he was accepted at the University of California at Berkeley, he dropped out after only one week, once more got caught up in what he refers to as "the scene," and never returned to school.

"I was pretty unmotivated for the first few years out of high school, up until the time I was twenty," Danny says. He went from one menial job to another, even working as a bicycle messenger and selling chandeliers for minimum wage, until he became more goal-oriented in 1972. While working a clerical job at Billboard magazine, the trade publication for the music business, he found his true love and has been connected with the music business ever since.

When Danny was twenty-two, he took a job at a public relations firm, developed an interest in spiritual ideas, and began attending weekly meditations. The most important thing he took from meditation, he says, is learning to "stay in the moment. If you can place a value on what you are doing in the moment, it makes life easier. Forget about getting the immediate reward. You are able to get the reward somewhere down the line if you persist moment by moment, experience by experience. One moment at a time, one hour at a time, and one day at a time, do those things you need to do and the answers will guide you. Often the work you are doing is not fun, but if you try to infuse as much energy as possible into the experience, you will make headway toward your vision."

The PR firm he was working for had a number of prestigious clients including Barbra Streisand and Frank Sinatra, and although Danny didn't deal directly with those "stars," he did personally handle Led Zeppelin, a relationship that was pivotal to kick-starting his subsequent career. Everyone who worked at the company had a very strong work ethic, and Danny, too, began to embrace the idea of working hard. Of course, he had also been out of work for a few months at that time and, as he said, "Lack of money can make you redefine what's important to you and make you more agreeable to the system."

In 1976 he formed his first company, a move he laughingly says he made "so that I would stop getting fired." He enjoyed and thrived on his independence for the next fourteen years, but when he got married at the age of forty and had his first child, he realized that his priorities had changed. He wanted security for his family, and although he had done well on his own, he hadn't saved his money, and he felt a new sense of responsibility. And, in addition, being in business for himself took an enormous amount of time and energy, often requiring him to be in the office seven days a week, and he now wanted to spend more time at home.

In the years that followed, Danny held positions as Chairman and CEO of Warner Bros. Records, Chairman and CEO of the Mercury Records Group, and President of Atlantic Records. During those years he worked with Madonna, Neil Young, REM, and Phil Collins. Artists signed under his various regimes included Shania Twain, Boyz II Men, Hanson, Elvis Costello, Jewel, Brandy, and Hootie and the Blowfish.

But in 1999, on the heels of his corporate successes, Danny went independent again, forming Artemis Records, of which he is Chairman and CEO. Less than a year after its creation, Artemis had placed four albums on the charts, and in 2000, "Who Let the Dogs Out" became the biggest selling independently distributed album in the United States.

Danny credits much of his success to having great intuition and the guts to follow it, but he also says he's been lucky. He believes that some force beyond his understanding is protecting him, and he trusts his path. He says that he's made innumerable personal and professional mistakes as well as decisions he wouldn't recommend to anyone, but ultimately, they've panned out!

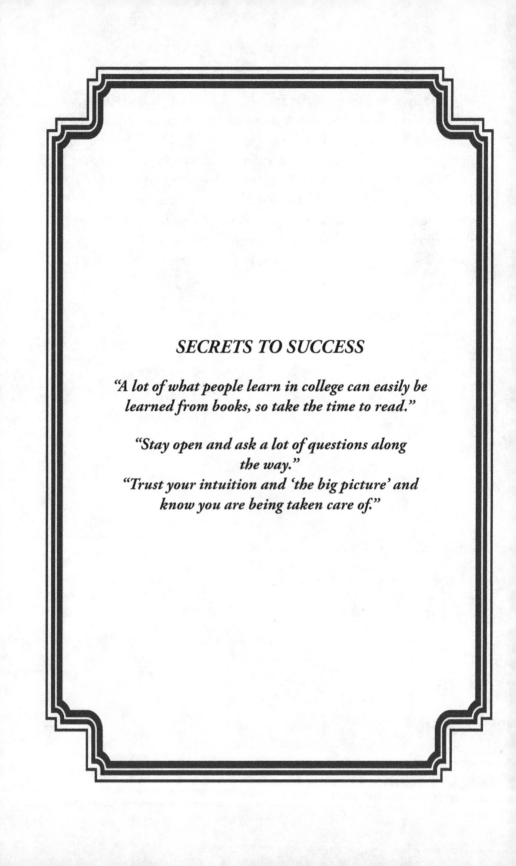

SECRETS TO SUCCESS

*"A lot of what people learn in college can easily be
learned from books, so take the time to read."*

*"Stay open and ask a lot of questions along
the way."*

*"Trust your intuition and 'the big picture' and
know you are being taken care of."*

'HOW TO' BE SUCCESSFUL

The key to success is doing what you love to do. You have probably heard "do what you love to do and the money will follow". I believe that is true. The first task is to figure out what it is you love to do and what you can bring to the world through doing the thing you love to do.

Here are five questions you can ask yourself:

1. *What was I born to do?*
2. *What do I love to do?*
3. *What is important to me?*
4. *What am I good at?*
5. What benefit am I uniquely equipped to provide to the world?

You may be saying to yourself, fine, that is all well and good but how do I figure this out.

Following are a few exercises you can do to discover your talents.

1. Buy a small notebook. Carry it with you. Whenever you feel that you are engaged in a conversation that stimulates you, excites you, keeps your interest, write down the topic.
2. Browse through magazines and newspapers, even note the books that you like to read and write down what interests you the most. Even if you just like to read "People" Magazine, that is giving you a clue. You may like fashion, you may like star gossip, you may like reporting on people, you may like the photographs, you may like the interaction between people, whatever it is, these are clues to what you love to do. By the same token, if you love to watch car races or always talk about

To order DEGREES OF SUCCESS, view live interviews, blog or contact Claudia Fox: Go to www.thefoxwayworks.com

sports, there is something in there for you. Nothing is too small to write down. The answer is in the details.

3. Go on the Internet and look at job sites. Careerbuilders.com is just one that is filled with all kinds of information. See what interests you, see what qualifications are necessary for things that interest you.

4. When you watch television or go to the movies, listen to music, whatever you are doing in the day, check in with yourself and see what pleases you, what brings you joy. It might be new for you to even consider having joy in the day. Usually our noses are to the grindstone and we forget what it is like to just have fun or be playful.

5. Do you like to exercise, play sports, dance or do any other physical thing? This is the time to write it down. No one else is going to see this so you can just write to your heart's content.

6. Think about what made you happy as a child. Even go back and look at some photos of your youth. Not all of us remember a lot of happy times, we tend to remember the worst anyway, but there might have been some things that made you feel a sense of joy. Write those down.

You still may be stopped. Continue with these exercises:

Ask the people around you, friends, family, people at work, what they think you are good at – write that down. While you are at it, also ask them for some weaknesses. Tell them that you will not be mad at them for telling the truth, and don't be mad at them. You can tell them this will be very useful to you in finding out what you want to do in life. This can also help you figure out what some of the blocks to having what you want are.

You can ask these questions:

1. *What are my strengths?*
2. *What are my weaknesses?*
3. *What do people know that I can be counted on for?*
4. *What do people say I am not willing to do?*
5. *How would you describe the things I do well?*

To order DEGREES OF SUCCESS, view live interviews, blog or contact Claudia Fox:
Go to www.thefoxwayworks.com

Now you should be starting to get some good clues. If you are still stopped, I suggest you call a career coach and take an hour or so to get some help determining what you are good at and enjoy doing to create a career path for yourself. If you have a large block and you know it, get a recommendation for a good therapist and do what it takes to get through the issues that are holding you back. Having a person listen and guide you toward your success is an incredible journey. I believe in the buddy system, even if you don't need or want a therapist. Enroll a friend or join a group (or even create your own group) that will commit to definite actions each week and join it. You can contact me my website for recommendations. See below.

Perhaps you are one of those people who have always known what you want to do and just don't feel that you have the money, the time or the self-confidence to do it. You are a few steps ahead of the game because you know what you are meant to be doing and just haven't yet done it. Don't beat yourself up, consider that NOW is the right time to get involved in your purpose in life. It's never too late to get started. I have known people in their 60's and even 80's who start over. We all come to it at different times.

Now go into www.google.com and look up some of things you like to do. Put in subjects that interest you to see what comes up. Are there things you can get involved in. Are there people there for you to see. See what businesses are created from your interests. You may want to work for someone to get started even though you most likely want your own business if you are reading this or you may even have a bent toward non-profit.

Start a practice of writing each morning, hopefully you can do this on your computer, but many have done it by writing in a notebook. Start the stream of negativity and fears. The idea for this came from the book called " The Artist's Way" wherein you will find many exercises that will stimulate your creativity. Type or write down all the things that bothered you yesterday, are going to bother you today and will continue to bother you tomorrow. Type or write at least three full pages each morning. The wonderful thing is that the more garbage you write about, the more you free you mind up to let new and positive ideas come in during the day. I did this exercise once for a full month and when I was done I began writing poetry I never even knew was inside of me. I mean, great poetry, that even my husband's aunt was buried with (my husband loved it so much) and I even wrote some songs. It is amazing what comes out when the negativity is dispelled.

At night before you go to sleep, write down ten things you are grateful for. This allows your mind to go to sleep and rest in a positive frame of mind. Avoid the news before you go to bed. If you have to read about all the bad things happening in the world, do it during the day or night when you get home in the early evening, not before you go to bed.

You are doing well by now, at discovering or having known the thing or things you love to do, and by the way if there are more than one, you may have to do some research to see which thing is more timely now or what fits in with what is going on in the world or most importantly what is the most important to you.

Another thing you might want to consider is meditation once or twice a day. I find this invaluable. I took the Transcendental Meditation course in my twenties and have been doing it ever since. It helps to keep you youthful - no one that thinks I am my age. It has also helped that I eat right, do not drink or smoke and stay away from sugar, as much as possible. I know for some of you this is daunting but you have to take a look at what blocks your moving forward. Perhaps you need a 12-step program to get rid of some addiction. That could be anything that takes you away from being in the present. There are programs for alcoholics, spouses or mates of alcoholics, children of alcoholics, debtors and drug addicts. You must do something now if you are going around in circles from an addiction. The 12-step programs are all over the world and they are free. Many wonderful costly programs use the same methodology but you can have practical daily support for a small donation. Or for free, if need be. There is miraculous recovery in the rooms.

There are other programs that are more costly but the lessons are great and the networking incredible. Landmark Education at www. landmarkeducation.com has incredible break-through courses – to this day I still keep myself involved in a seminar so that I can always be around evolving people and a positive conversation. Robert Allen, real estate mogul and author who wrote "Cracking the Millionaire Code" runs an incredible group called Enlightened Wealth Institute. His retreats, when I took them, were free and from there you are invited to join other courses which are not free but well worth the investment. You can reach him through their web-site www.crackingthemillionairecode. com or call them on the West Coast at 1 801 852 8700. (Remember the three hour time difference). I found them to be incredibly supportive and I took countless hour-long courses during my week while I was writing and marketing my book. Whatever the next step was, there just seemed to be a great course with a great teacher. I am still connected to people who are outstanding in their fields of work.

For free, you can watch a TV show called "THE BIG IDEA" with Donny Deutsch where he listens to your innovative ideas and inventions and helps connect you to people who can help you. He has a panel that expresses their opinion about your project. He has people on who started out with nothing and ended up with millions. I love this show and it has become part of my educational process. In my area, New York, it is on every night at 10PM.

Also for those of you who have inventions, you can check out "the Mom Inventors Handbook" by Tamara Monosoff, you don't have to be a Mom to use it. I have an idea for an invention and got perfect information for what I want to do. They are also available to coach.

And one of the most important parts of my day is prayer. We cannot ever underestimate the power of prayer. If you have not seen "What the Bleep Do We Know", get yourself to one of the video stores and rent it. This documentary shows how powerful our words are. I believe in the power of prayer as well as positive affirmations. I have made some up and have taken some from the "Game of Life" by Florence Scovell Shinn, who I think is brilliant and has a firm grip on life. I pray all of the time, I pray for others and I pray for myself. "Miracle will follow miracle and wonders will never cease, today is the day of miracles" is one of my favorites". If I am in a negative mood, sometimes I will say this over and over until I come out of the mood.. I also watch Joel Osteen who is a young preacher and is on late in the evening and I just love that I am going to sleep with a spiritual feeling and positive input. He is very practical and talks about how important it is to think positive. He has created a church following through the television and his latest book called He also has best seller books out that I have not read but think would be valuable.

One of the things I remind myself is that I have spent a lifetime justifying negative thoughts and it may take the rest of my lifetime to create thoughts anew and put something purposeful and positive into my mind. I can't tell you enough that the words you hear in your head are powerful and will lead you down one path or another. It's not what people say to you, it's what you say to yourself about what they are saying. I believe you are what you believe in and think about. Watch your thoughts, have you ever noticed that your fears come true, that is because that is what you are thinking about. Change your thoughts and you will change your life.

Regarding work you may want to work part-time at your new found purpose while you are working full time. You may be able to work full time on your purpose and part time to support yourself. You may be lucky enough to be supported. You can also go out and volunteer and get into your career of interest that way.

You can start your research by getting a mentor. Ask five friends if they know of someone in your career of interest. Get their numbers and go interview them. You should keep asking until you interview at least six people. As them the following questions:

1. *What are your current responsibilities?*
2. *What was your career path?*
3. *What excites you about your position?*
4. *Did you always have drive and ambition?*
5. *How do you think you got it?*
6. *What skills do you use to do your job that make you passionate about your work?*
7. *What skills would someone need in order to work toward a position like yours?*
8. *What advice would you have for people who want to get into your field?*

Perhaps you can get a job there and start working in the area you love. Maybe they will even discover your talents and create a job for you. The most important thing is to start taking ACTIONS. Do you realize that if you take just one action a week by the end of the year you will have taken 52 actions toward you goal and look at what happens when you double your efforts - that would be 104 actions – that's incredible. And it's certainly way more than the nothing you have done so far.

You should do some more research at this point.

Pick out some people that you think are just plain ol' successful, like Bill Gates, Peter Jennings and read their biographies. Learn what made them continue on through their obstacles and adversities. I watched a movie called "Pumping Iron" three times with Arnold Schwarzenegger and found that movie to be highly motivating. You can easily rent that at Blockbuster.

You may want to go back to school or go to a trade school. Consider these are possibilities and they all have to be worked into what you need to support yourself. But remember taking a few steps each week even though it may take years to accomplish your goal is certainly better than just thinking about it and one day realizing the time is gone.

Try to lead a balanced life, even if it seems impossible, but if you have tremendous surge of energy toward a project, just go for it. Some people say that they can work 20 hours a day without depleting their energy because they love what they are doing. There are no right and wrongs so you have to do what works for you. A good night's sleep will go a long way toward keeping your attitude shaped up. Although, there have been times when I am just so energized by a project, that I can't put it down. You may want to check with family members to see how they feel about that because you don't want to become successful and be alone. The idea here is to contribute to society, it's not just about having. I think I feel best when I eat right, get enough sleep, exercise and have fun doing things that fill my soul along with loving what I do. For instance, I love to dance. It takes me away from everything that I might consider worrying about. The music allows me to float around without thinking and learning new steps keeps my mind focused.

To order DEGREES OF SUCCESS, view live interviews, blog or contact Claudia Fox:
Go to www.thefoxwayworks.com

Some books are great to read a bit each day. They even have books that tell you what to read on a specific day of the week. I like these because I know that I am going to be reading the same thing as a whole group of people will be reading on any given day and that makes me feel connected. These can help to set the tone of your day. You can listen to "Affluence" Deepak Chopra – I have had some amazing miracles happen to me listening to this CD I in my car. It also taught me the basic principles of money.

Stop worrying about what others think! If you know that you keep doing the same thing over and over and are like a mouse going down that path without the cheese, get off your duff and do something about it. There is help everywhere. Here are some additional things to consider:

Visualization - Sit quietly and picture the end goal. Really go through the details and imagine yourself in the situation you want to be in. For instance, when I visualize, I see myself standing before audiences talking about being successful. I have been told the mind cannot tell the difference between the real or imagined so you will be setting the scene for future experiences.

Networking – Get yourself out there. Find groups that are doing what you are doing and mingle with those people. Exchange ideas. Rarely do things happen in a vacuum. Yes, it is good to think about things but ultimately you are going to have to take some actions to get things done. Other people are a great resource. They have a new pair of eyes and come up with creative ideas I would never have thought of. You must learn to do this anyway because once you get your project going, the only way to get it out to the universe is through people.

Tithing – I believe if you have a good cause and a philanthropic mind, you will receive everything you need in order to attain your goal. I give 10% of everything I make to the organizations in the back of my book. It makes me feel good and it certainly has helped a lot of people. My most memorable times have been helping others. It just gives me a warm feeling. At other times, I give of my time. For the Hurricane Katrina victims, I invited them on my show, I collected clothes for them and I am cooking up another project for them as we speak. Most recently I ran a bowling charity event for the Northern Westchester Shelter with Stephen Paletta, Oprah Big-Give winner of $1 million dollars, along with my husband who so kindly donated his bowling alley, Cortlandt Lanes, in Cortlandt, New York, for the event. I tracked Stephen down through the internet and called him. Yes, just like that. . . . and he so graciously offered to help. He even brought his wife and three daughters to bowl! I believe that the universe does support such endeavors and your rewards are many.

Technology – Remember this is the age of technology. You must at least get a computer and know the basics. It is essential to have email and to be able to type. Get help if you are not there yet. There are so many classes, it could make your head spin. Pick a basic one. You don't have to create a web-site, there are some things you will just have to pay for. A web-site may be one of them. If you have money, you can hire people to do things, if not, you will have to figure out to do some of these things yourself.

Set goals – Figure out where you want to be in five years, back it up by year until you get to one year. Then start getting more detailed. Figure out what it takes to reach your goals, go month by month until you get to now. This is where having picked someone else's brain will be so helpful. You really want to know what steps you have to take to get to where you want to go. And of course, start taking the actions.

Expect setbacks – It always happens and the people who are successful go back to the drawing board and figure out what to do. Don't get down and if you do, call someone who can get you back up. I have such a person. Her name is Debbie Bern, my therapist. I can always count on her to get me back into forward motion. The failures are the things that teach us what to do to get the project done. We have to learn from them. Sometimes, we discover the perfect thing that will put our project on the map.

Expect a Miracle – Can you imagine a day where you did not think there was a miracle in it? Just being human is a miracle in and of itself. Being able to talk, to walk and think. These are all miracles. Try saying "The miracles appear for me to see" and see what happens. I will make a believer out of you yet.

To order DEGREES OF SUCCESS, view live interviews, blog or contact Claudia Fox:
Go to www.thefoxwayworks.com

GIVE BACK BY TITHING

To tithe is to donate 10 percent of one's income to doing good works. Until attending a course given by Robert G. Allen, author of Nothing Down, and Multiple Streams of Income, and Mark Victor Hansen, co-author of Chicken Soup for the Soul, I had thought about tithing, but had never actually made the commitment.

Upon leaving their course, however, I sold my cooperative apartment and tithed ten percent of the profits from the sale. A portion went to FlowerPower, a portion to my church mission, a portion to Leukemia and Lymphoma (for which my brother, George, jogged, swam and biked a 26.5-mile marathon) and a portion to the Dream Center in California. Doing that was such a wonderful experience that it filled my heart with joy. To give is to promote spirituality—in yourself and in the world.

If you are moved to tithe, following are some special organizations that do wonderful deeds in the world and information about how you can reach them. I also highly recommend that you read Mark Victor Hansen's The Miracle of Tithing, which can be ordered online from www.markvictorhansen.com.

Do Something, Inc.

Lezlie Wheeler,
COO 24-32 Union Square East,
4th Floor New York,
NY 10003

Tel: 212 254 2390 x227
Fax: 212 254 2391
E-mail: lwheeler@dosomething.org
www.dosomething.org

Do Something, Inc. celebrates and unleashes the power of young people to take action and change their world. We believe every kid can do something to impact their world. It is our job to make sure that they have the role models, resources and mentors to help them do something.

We help young people change their world by giving them the inspiration and opportunity to do something to make a difference. When kids are active citizens, they develop lifelong leadership skills and character.

Pajama Program

Genevieve Piturro
116 East 27th Street
New York, New
York 10016

Tel: 212 716 9757
www.pajamaprogram.org

The Pajama Program provides warm pajamas and nurturing books to needy children, many of whom are waiting and hoping to be adopted. They are youngsters who do not know the comforts of a mother or father to tuck them into a cozy bed and read them a bedtime story. Many have been abandoned or abused, most have been deprived of any love at all.

Fostering Futures

Kim Law
P. O. Box 184
Reddick,
FL 32686

Tel: 352 591 3339
www.yourfamiliesfuture.com

Fostering Futures empowers people through education, hands-on training, and life skills workshops to help families succeed and thrive in life, giving them the knowledge and experience necessary to prosper throughout their lives. We positively effect the lives of generations past and generations to come.

Rural Education and Development

Dr. Vijaya Nair
1 Smith Road
Bedford, New
York 10506

Tel: 914 234 2150
E-mail: Vvn2@columbia.net

Rural Education and Development (READ) is an international not-for-profit humanitarian program working with indigenous peoples to increase literacy and promote economic development, primarily in lesser developed nations. Among its humanitarian endeavors, READ has thus far built 50 libraries in rural and remote areas of Nepal, and has just dedicated the first of many in India where READ is now focusing much of its time, effort, and expense. Having received recognition from several charitable and philanthropic organizations, including the United Nations and the Bill & Melinda Gates Foundation (READ is the 2008 recipient of the Gates "Access to Learning" award), READ is determined to now take its program into five more countries in the developing world in the next three years.

Please see info on READGLOBAL: www.readglobal.org regarding donations.

Anselma House

Anne Tilley
P. O. Box 32008
Cambridge,
Ontario NSH5M2

Tel: Free 1 877 419 1517
www.wcswr.org

The Staff and Board of Directors of Anselma House/Haven House are committed to providing a safe and supportive environment for physically, sexually, and emotionally abused women and their children. They believe the design and provision of direct and indirect service programs will effect a better society. Their global vision for the future is a society where violence is eradicated and there is no longer a need for shelters to protect women and children from violence.

A NOTE FROM THE AUTHOR

If you would like your favorite charity to be included in future versions of my book, please list the organization's name, address, person to contact, and a telephone number or e-mail address at:

www.thefoxwayworks.com

You can order the book on the website. You will find information, such as courses, recommendations and other related information.

I would love to receive your success stories. You can e-mail them to me through the website or at claudia@thefoxwayworks.com

CLAUDIA LOGAN FOX

Claudia Fox has a stellar reputation as a one-on-one coach, group trainer, sales team trainer and presentation coach who offers confidence, patience and enthusiasm to every individual and group she works with. She has evaluated, coached and trained thousands of individuals, many of them executives who have attained higher level careers who were able to recognize valuable contributions they could make by transferring their skills and talents to new companies. More than 90 percent of her clients have increased their salary packages by using negotiation skills that she taught them.

In addition to coaching executives and brokers, Claudia has also coached teens who were not college bound to attain a great understanding of the options available to them, specifically at Mt. Vernon High School in Mt. Vernon, New York where in the past, she has developed and led workshops. These workshops address career assessment, career exposure, resume writing, networking and interviewing skills as well as interview role playing. She has also involved the community by encouraging them to provide shadowing and mentoring positions for prospective part and full-time job openings for the teens.

Formerly a motivational trainer with PSE&G's "Effective Learning Systems," Claudia has an extensive history in real estate sales training. She has held positions such as President of Zeckendorf's "Manhattan Sales", Executive Associate for the Trump Organization in New York City and Career Advisor for Bernard Haldane Associates in Tarrytown, New York. "My experience in the real estate industry includes selecting, hiring and coaching the top 10 percent of real estate executives in the nation," says Claudia. She developed and led many training programs for the real estate industry, including one for a very successful project on the Upper West Side of Manhattan that resulted in the sale of 75% of the properties that were sold within six weeks of entering the marketplace.

Claudia Fox was interviewed by Marsha Gordon, President of the Westchester Business Council about her career business services. The interview was aired on WVOX. She was also featured on Peekskill's New York cablevision show "Healthscope" talking about the affects corporate downsizing has had on executives. She co-hosted a cablevision show called "Turn Your Passion into Profit" which aired in White Plains, New York, every Monday and Friday nights at 8:30PM for two years running where she interviewed people who were passionate about their careers.

Claudia's charitable goal is to create a foundation to support teens who are going to trade schools.

NOTES

CPSIA information can be obtained
at www.ICGtesting.com
Printed in the USA
BVHW031354021120
592327BV00016B/480/J